THE INDEF
GUIDE TO
TOKYO
2021

G. COSTA

Contents

An Important Message Regarding the Global Pandemic:

At the time we were updating this guide , most of the world was under quarantine due to the global pandemic. As Tokyo reopens, the government is understandably cautious about how it will make visits safe for everyone. In the short term, at least, your visits may be affected by enhanced crowd control and social distancing measures and the possible cancellation (or changes) to shows, attractions, dining experiences, transportation and other experiences. The Tokyo 2020 Olympics has, at the time of writing, been rescheduled to take place from Friday, 23 July to Sunday, 8 August 2021.

Tokyo: A Brief History

Tokyo is endlessly rewarding to those who take the time to get to know it. Before we explore, let's look back at Tokyo's past to understand how it became the city it is today.

Fishing Village to Fortifications: Pre-History to Heian period

It's hard to imagine Tokyo was once a collection of tiny fishing villages.

The Imperial Family first appeared in 300 AD, when the Yamato family established a capital in Nara Prefecture. Buddhism arrived in Japan from China, bringing with it Chinese laws and writing, powerful influences on Japanese society.

In what is now Tokyo, in 628 AD, two brothers founded and built a Buddhist temple in the fishing village of Asakusa, which quickly became a pilgrimage site.

The Imperial family established a new capital in Kyoto, ushering in the Heian period (794-1185). The Edo clan took control of Tokyo towards the end of the Heian period, building a residence on the site of today's Imperial Palace.

The Edo-clan strengthened their position with military defenses, but were unable to keep control of their base, now known as 'Edo.'

Warring States Period: Edo Changes Hands

As the Imperial family's position was weakened by rival claimants to the throne, the daimyo took advantage to seize military power for themselves.

A succession of military leaders, styling themselves shogun, held increasing amounts of power, while the Imperial family became more of a figurehead.

Skirmishes between daimyo anxious to seize even more power became more frequent, culmination in the Warring States period, a time of intense fighting lasting from 1467-1603 AD.

Edo Period: Tokyo Blossoms

The Tokugawa shogunate ruled Japan during the Edo period from 1603-1868 AD.

Although the Imperial family remained in Kyoto, the official capital, the Emperor's power was purely ceremonial. Edo was the true military, political and financial capital, and developed a thriving culture that quickly rivaled Kyoto's. Buildings were primarily built of wood and people lived in crowded conditions along tiny, twisty streets.

Fires were a constant source of danger. Life was hard, but gave rise to a flourishing counter culture.

To keep a firm hold on the reins of power, the Tokugawa shoguns demanded that the feudal lords spend alternate years in Edo. The city's population grew, making it the biggest city in the world in 1725 with a population of 1.1 million people—but devastated the feudal lords.

The Tokugawa shoguns segregated Japan from the rest of the world. Trade was strictly controlled, and contact with foreigners was only allowed at designated trading ports.

In 1868, Commodore Perry sailed into Tokyo Bay at the head of a fleet of gun-boats, demanding that Japan open itself to the world.

In 1867-8, Emperor Meiji assumed power.

Meiji Restoration: Enlightened Tokyo

Emperor Meiji moved the Imperial household to Edo Castle and renamed Edo to 'East Capital'—Tokyo. Foreign ideas and innovations flooded into Japan's capital city. The Meiji Restoration lasted from 1868-1912, and saw militarization and industrialization in Japan.

The feudal class system was abolished, and the Emperor and his advisors instituted wide-ranging reforms along Western models. Tokyo changed dramatically. Western building styles were popular, adopted by the government to foster Japan's image as a modern country, while its people adopted Western haircuts and clothing.

Shinto was adopted as the national religion with the Emperor, a living god, at its center.

Japan's military made forays into Korean, Chinese, and Russian territory.

Disaster: Tokyo Devastated

On September 1st 1923, a 7.9 magnitude earthquake took place in Sagami Bay. The earthquake resulted in widespread fires which took three days to bring under control, at which point 142,800 people were dead.

Tokyo was in ruins. Military rule was briefly declared. Tokyo however wasted no time getting back to business. Parks were planned as evacuation spots, while roads and trains replaced Tokyo's former, tiny, twisting streets. Many of the buildings and shrines that survived the earthquake did not survive WWII. Tokyo was the target of frequent American air-raids. Half of Tokyo's population fled the city and a quarter of the capital's buildings were destroyed.

Tokyo became the base of the American occupying forces from 1945-1951. The reforms of the Meiji-era

continued, and the Emperor's power was weakened, leading to the Imperial family's largely ceremonial role today.

Tokyo Rebuilds: After the Bubble Burst

Tokyo once more rose from the ashes to invent itself as a modern city with the hosting of the 1964 Olympics.

Tokyo saw a myriad of construction as stadiums, hotels and subway systems were built which demonstrated Tokyo's status as a modern city.

The success of the Olympics led to an increase in national pride and went some way to soothing the wounds left from Japan's WWII defeat. It also heralded Japan's return as a global superpower.

Tokyo continued to develop, going from strength to strength. The high cost of land and the need for housing and office space gave rise to the skyscrapers that now dominate Tokyo. The 1980s, the height of Japan's bubble economy, fuelled the city's rapid development. New business centers sprang up throughout Tokyo, to meet the growing needs of its expanding population.

Today: Changing Tokyo

Following the collapse of the bubble economy and the global economic downturn, Japan entered a period of two recessions, from which it has yet to fully recover. Efforts to rebuild were hampered by the 2011 Tohoku earthquake.

As the city prepares for the 2021 Olympics, redevelopment continues at a rapid pace. Ambitious plans to once again reinvent the city and establish it on the global stage are underway. As the city gears up to put on an incredible show there is no better time to visit Tokyo, and witness the city's power of reinvention for yourself.

Know Before You Go

Before getting into all the fantastic things to do, places to stay and locations to dine, we will look at what makes Tokyo so unique. This section covers key aspects you should know before your visit.

Local Customs and Etiquette

Underneath the superficial resemblance to New York or parts of London, Tokyo is a city with a culture that is distinctly Japanese. Only a few blocks away from glitzy skyscrapers are run-down apartment blocks, and the occasional rice field or vegetable garden still remains in use today in the outer suburbs.

Another contradiction that traps foreign tourists is Japan's attitude to money. Many visitors are caught out by ATMs that only open from 9:00-17:00, or shops that don't accept credit cards. Japan is primarily a cash-based society still, and has been slow to adopt internet banking and 24/7 ATMs. The situation is improving, but for the time being, get used to carrying cash. You can relax though—Tokyo's incredibly low crime rates make carrying cash a safe option.

Instead of trying to figure out Tokyo's many contradictions, embrace the mishmash of ideas and cultures as an integral part of what makes Tokyo the fascinating city it is today.

People

Japan is incredibly homogenous, even today. Only 3% of Japan's population is non-Japanese. The reason for this is Japan's strict immigration policies. Although it is very difficult to become a resident of Japan, the Japanese are very welcoming to visitors, often going to great lengths to help tourists. Tokyo has the highest population of English speakers in the country, but even when residents don't speak much English, they will do their best to help you. Don't be afraid to ask for directions from passersby.

It is difficult for Japanese people to find opportunities to practice their English, so many are keen to talk to foreign visitors. Popular topics include the weather and what you think of Japan. Be tactful! Japanese people have a lot of pride in their country, and don't take criticism of it well. Unless invited to speak about the

topic, mentioning the sensitive subject of whaling, dolphin hunting, or Japan's WWII involvement is heavily discouraged.

Visitors may also be overwhelmed by the level of politeness they receive in Japan! Shops, particularly department stores, and restaurant staff obey strict rules of politeness, adopting *keigo*, a highly stylized polite form of Japanese, to greet customers and conduct business. If you don't understand what's going on, request 'easy Japanese' or simply smile—staff will not be offended if you don't understand.

Although English education is a big part of Japan's school curriculum, many shy Japanese struggle to master English. Once you leave the tourist destinations and start exploring Tokyo, people are less confident in their English speaking ability. If you step into a shop and the

assistant immediately disappears, don't be offended! They've probably gone to find someone with better English skills to assist you.

Author Note: *"Keep in mind cultural differences when communicating! I once asked for directions at Ueno station and was told to take the 'tea-colored line.' As I walked towards the brown-colored train line, my helper ran after me. 'No, the tea-colored line,' he said, pointing to the green Yamanote platform."*

When to Visit: National Holidays & Weather

Japan's peak tourist times differ from the rest of the world. During peak tourist time, hotel prices go up and trains and buses may be fully booked well in advance. It's worth taking Japanese holidays into account when making your travel plans.

The major times to be aware of are the sakura season (late March-early April) when parks known for cherry-blossoms are packed with visitors; Golden Week, a string of national holidays at the end of April/early May; Obon, a week in August when families travel to tend to their ancestral graves; and the New Year's period, where most of Tokyo's museums and restaurants shut down. Plus, there are these holidays:

National Holidays in Japan 2021			
January 1st	New Year's Day	**July 19th**	Marine Day
January 11th	Coming of Age Day	**August 11th**	Mountain Day
February 11th	National Foundation Day	**September 20th**	Respect for the Aged Day
March 20th	Vernal Equinox	**September 23rd**	Autumn Equinox
April 29th	Showa Day	**October 11th**	Health/Sports Day
May 3rd	Constitution Memorial Day	**November 3rd**	Culture Day
May 4th	Greenery Day	**November 23rd**	Labour Thanksgiving Day
May 5th	Children's Day	**February 23rd**	Emperor's Birthday

Tokyo's weather varies dramatically season to season. The best times to visit are during Spring and Fall when the more mellow weather makes for comfortable traveling, and produces beautiful scenery. At peak cherry blossom or autumn time, popular parks can become extremely crowded.

Spring
Japan becomes obsessed with cherry blossoms. Tokyo's sakura usually bloom around the end of March or early April. Spring temperatures range from 6-22°C during the day. There is a second short rainy season in spring, but apart from occasional showers, the weather is generally good. Beware of traveling in early May. Golden Week, a string of national holidays, is an incredibly popular time for Japanese people to travel.

Summer
Summer is time for the Obon festival where families travel home to tend to their ancestral graves. It's also the time for fireworks festivals and summer festivals, and is uncomfortably humid, particularly during June and July - Japan's rainy season.

It's worth investing in a good umbrella as raincoats are uncomfortable in Tokyo's summer heat.

Summer temperatures range from 19-32°C during the day, but the humidity means it feels much warmer. Make sure to stay hydrated and keep cool.

Autumn/Fall
Autumn is when the bulk of Japan's school holidays take place, so family-orientated attractions are extremely crowded.

Tokyo sees a second rainy season in fall, as frequent typhoons lash the capital with strong rain and wind. The days following a typhoon are incredibly calm and fine, perfect exploring weather.

Towards the end of fall, the autumn foliage draws visitors to Tokyo's parks. Numerous events take advantage of the cooler temperatures, including the Tokyo Film Festival. In mid-November, keep an eye out for adorably dressed children heading to shrines for the *shichi-go-san* (3-5-7) festival. Autumn temperatures range from 9-27°C during the day.

Winter

Snow in Tokyo is relatively rare, and the weather tends to be crisp rather than chilly. The New Years' period is busy as the businesses end the year with *bonnenkai*, a lavish party. Japanese people celebrate Christmas with friends or dates (if at all) and travel home to spend the New Year period with their family.

Like *Obon* and Golden Week, New Year is a peak travel time in Japan. The many traditions surrounding the New Year make this a fun time to visit Tokyo, but be careful to make your travel arrangements well in advance to ensure that you don't end up stranded. Daytime temperatures range from 2-12°C.

Weather Averages by Month - First in Celsius, then in Fahrenheit in brackets					
January	2-8 (36-46)	**May**	14-21 (57-70)	**September**	20-26 (68-79)
February	2-9 (26-48)	**June**	18-24 (64-75)	**October**	15-20 (59-68)
March	5-12 (41-54)	**July**	22-28 (72-82)	**November**	9-15 (48-59)
April	10-17 (50-63)	**August**	23-29 (73-84)	**December**	4-11 (39-52)

Takyubin Luggage Service

Takyubin is a luggage delivery service available all over Japan. From Narita or Haneda airports, you can have your heavy suitcases delivered directly to your hotel for as little as ¥1,500. Within Tokyo, the service offers next-day delivery and makes traveling Tokyo's trains and buses easy. Pack your carry-on luggage with everything you'll need for your first day in Tokyo, and send the rest of your luggage on from the airport, or any major station. When you leave or transfer to a different hotel, do the same thing. Most hotel desks have the forms to fill out. You can write the address in kanji or in Roman letters. For more information, check out Kuroneko Takyubin at kuronekoyamato.co.jp/en.

Navigating Tokyo

Japanese addresses operate very differently to Western addresses. Tokyo city is divided by wards, and those wards into districts, neighborhoods and blocks. Those blocks are further divided. As an example: 〒111-0032 東京都台東区浅草2-3-1 (2-3-1 Asakusa, Taito-ku, Tokyo Postcode: 111-0032)

Taken apart, the address reads 東京都(Tokyo-city), 台東区(Taito-ward), 浅草 (Asakusa-district) 2-3-1 (Neighborhood 2, block 3, building 1).

Taken in combination with Tokyo's crowded and often not signposted streets, the result is a confusing maze that it is easy to get lost in. Tokyo's major attractions are easy enough. Follow the signs from major train stations, and, when you're close, follow the other tourists to your destination. For lesser-visited attractions, it is better to allow yourself extra time to get there.

A smartphone makes all the difference in navigating Tokyo - Google and Apple Maps work well.

A 4G/Wi-Fi rental service is very useful and the cost entirely repays itself in time saved working out how best to navigate Tokyo's streets and public transport networks.

There are a number of websites with information, timetables, routes and costs for Tokyo's public transport options. The best is hyperdia.com/en which covers all of Japan. Train stations must be entered exactly as the Hyperdia system has them listed. Try entering the first few letters of the station name and wait for its suggestions.

Google Maps and Apple Maps also include Tokyo's public transport options, and we find them to be reliable.

Getting to Tokyo
Flying

By far the most convenient way for international visitors to arrive in Tokyo is by plane. Tokyo is connected to the world by its two International Airports.

Upon arrival in Japan, visitors must endure a strict immigration process that includes a fingerprint check

and photo; this may lead to long queues at immigration. To be sure that you don't miss connecting trains, allow yourself an hour or more here.

Once through, if you plan on collecting a Japan Rail Pass, allow yourself even more time.

Narita Airport

Narita Airport is the older of Tokyo's two airports, and has the majority of international flights. It is 68 km from Tokyo Station. It has recently added a third terminal to accommodate budget airlines within Japan. Terminals One and Two are connected to Tokyo by a variety of train and bus options that take travelers directly to transport hubs Tokyo, Nippori, Ueno and Shinagawa. To get to Terminal Three, you must first reach Terminal Two and transfer via the courtesy shuttle bus or a short walk along the well-marked connecting pathway.

Public Transport
Narita Airport is well linked with public transport. The transfer option that works best for you may well depend on where you will be staying while in Tokyo.

Rail: Narita Express – Japan
Rail (JR) is Japan's national railway line. The JR Narita Express links Narita Airport directly to Tokyo Station with a journey time of 53 minutes. Trains depart every 30 minutes, starting at 07:44

from Narita Airport Terminal 1, and go until 21:44. You can also catch the Narita Express from Shinagawa, Shibuya, Shinjuku, Ikebukuro and Yokohama.

All seats on the Narita Express are reserved, so tickets must be bought in advance. At peak times, trains may fill up. Book in advance if you're concerned.

A one-way ticket costs ¥3,070 from Tokyo to Narita, but a round-trip ticket is only ¥4,070, and can be purchased at Narita Airport Terminals 1 and 2 from either the JR East Travel Service Center or the JR Ticket Office. The ticket is good for 14 days, making it perfect for most visitors. The ticket includes transfers on JR lines within the Tokyo metropolitan area.

Rail: Keisei Skyliner – The
Keisei line is a private railway line to Narita airport. Keisei Skyliner is the fastest way to reach Narita from Tokyo, taking 36 minutes from Nippori or 41 from Keisei-Ueno.

The Skyliner is linked to Shinagawa, Daiba, Shimbashi, Higashi-ginza, Nihombashi, Asakusa and Oshiage by the Keisei Access Express Line (which also goes to the Airport), making this a convenient option for travelers basing themselves in the Chuo and Minato areas.

Seats are reserved and tickets must be bought in advance. The first train from Narita departs at 07:28 (07:34 on weekends and holidays), and the final train leaves at 23:30.

A one-way ticket from Nippori/Ueno to Narita costs ¥2,520, or ¥2,250 if purchased in advance online or through an approved travel agency. A round-trip ticket is ¥5,040, or ¥4,380 purchased in advance.

The Keisei Skyliner ticket can also be purchased in combination with a Tokyo Subway pass for further savings, and can be purchased for a validity period of 24, 48 or 72 hours. These can be purchased online or via a travel agency.

Rail: Keisei Main Line – A cheaper rail option is to take the Keisei line from Ueno or Nippori to Narita Terminals one or two. A one-way ticket is ¥1,050 on the main line, or ¥1,270 on the slightly faster Narita Sky Access Line. Keep an eye on the time and the train schedule if you choose this option. The Keisei Line has local trains that stop at every station as well as limited expresses that only stop at a few main stations, leading to a big difference in journey time. The limited express takes 77 minutes, the local 94 minutes. The earliest departure on the Keisei line is at 05:16, and the last is at 22:49.

Bus: Limousine Bus – The limousine bus is one of the most convenient ways to travel, taking you directly from the airport to selected hotels. Limousine isn't a reference to the car, but a brand of buses that pride themselves on their quality and comfort.

You purchase the ticket before getting on the bus. You can buy tickets from the Narita Airport Limousine Bus Ticket Counter. A one-way ticket from Narita in to Tokyo is ¥2,800 (discounts are available online). A special discounted return voucher is available to foreign visitors only from the Narita Airport counter.

The downside to the convenience of the limousine bus is that Tokyo roads are crowded and, especially at peak times, congested. Without any traffic delays, the bus trip from central Tokyo to the airport takes about 50 minutes, but it can take up to 2 hours when traffic is bad. If you choose to take the bus, make sure you leave yourself plenty of time in case of delays. The earliest bus departs Narita Terminal 3 for Tokyo station at 08:45, and the last bus leaves at 18:10.

Airport Bus: TYO-NRT – Formerly called Access Narita, this is a discount bus option that takes you between Narita airport and Tokyo for only 1000 yen one-way. You board the bus and pay your fare in cash on the bus or online in advance at tyo-nrt.com. You can catch the bus from any of Narita's three terminals. Buses leave every 15 minutes during peak time, starting with the first bus departing terminal 3 at 07:30 and run until 23:00.

The trip from Ginza to Narita takes roughly 65-75 minutes, but this time is subject to change depending on traffic conditions. If taking this option, remember to leave yourself some extra time.

Special late night/early morning buses cost ¥2,000 per passenger.

Other Transport
Taxi – Tokyo has numerous taxi companies, and there is a taxi stand outside almost every station. Ahead of the Olympics, some taxi companies offer interpretation services in several languages, including English.

Taking a taxi may be convenient but it isn't cheap. Depending on traffic congestion, the ride from the city center to the airport takes between 60 to 90 minutes and costs between ¥20,000-25,000. Some taxis also require passengers to pay the highway tolls to the airport, increasing the fare.

Tokyo Narita Airport Shuttles – Narita airport is served by a number of airport shuttle companies, including Tokyo Limo, Super Shuttle, Blacklane, TT Shuttle and GO Airport Shuttle. All of these shuttles can be booked in advance through the conglomerate website, airportshuttles.com.

Fares range from about ¥40,000 for a vehicle for three people to ¥65,000 for the first-class service.

Rental Car – There are various rental car options available from Narita Airport, but driving in Tokyo is not recommended. In addition to the difficulties of navigating Tokyo's streets, parking is an issue. Drivers in Japan must provide proof of a parking space for their vehicle, so there are not a lot of free parking options and parking laws are strictly enforced. Overnight street parking is also illegal.

While some hotels and attractions have parking spaces for guests, these are limited. Unless you request a parking space when you book your hotel, you may find yourself out of luck.

Car rental agencies have desks at Terminal One and Two. To drive in Japan, you must obtain an International Drivers Permit, valid for 1 year, in your home country. travelers from Belgium, France, Germany, Monaco, Slovenia, Switzerland and Taiwan must obtain a translation of their driving license before driving.

25,000 YEN
= $250.00

Haneda Airport

Tokyo International Airport - or Haneda - is one of the busiest airports in Asia. The majority of flights are domestic, but increasing numbers of International flights are routed into Haneda. The airport is closer to the city than Narita, only 21 km from Tokyo Station. Haneda is well served by a variety of public transport options.

The international terminal is connected to the two domestic terminals by a free shuttle bus, and from there the numerous transport options.

Unfortunately, passengers arriving between 0:00 and 05:00 will find themselves looking at either a steep taxi fare or long wait as the public transport doesn't run during this period.

Public Transport
Rail: Monorail – The monorail takes you directly to and from Haneda's International Terminal in only thirteen minutes from Hamamatsucho Monorail station (which links up to JR and subway lines) and the International Terminal. The Monorail runs every 3 to 5 minutes, starting at 05:18 and running until 00:10 at night. You are allowed to take two items of luggage with a combined weight of 30 kg onto the monorail.

A one-way ticket between Hamamatsucho Station and the International Terminal is ¥500. As the monorail is so convenient for transfers, there are several combination tickets available to other destinations.

Rail: Keikyu Line – The Keikyu Line is a private railway line that links Haneda airport with Shinagawa and Yokohama. Travel between Shinagawa and the International Airport Terminal on the Airport Limited Express takes 11 minutes and costs ¥440 for a one-way ticket. Shinagawa station is a major transport hub, and you can easily transfer to the JR Lines or Subway System. The first train departs Haneda International Airport at 05:26, and the last departs at 00:02.

The Keikyu Line offers discount tickets for tourists, including Subway, Toie and Metro combination tickets.

Bus: Keihin Kyuko Limousine Bus – The Keikyu Line provides limousine buses to and from Haneda airport and a selection of hotels and major stations. Tickets must be purchased in advance from the Bus Ticket Sales Counter (left of the arrival gates in Haneda International Terminal), or from the bus ticket machines besides the bus stops.

The limousine bus has room for large items of luggage that can't be taken on the monorail or train. Limousine buses run to Tokyo, Yokohama, Osaki, Kashiwa and Kamata stations, or direct to some major tourist attractions, including the Tokyo Disney Resort and Tokyo Skytree.

The limousine bus is more comfortable and guarantees you a seat, but is more expensive and takes longer than the trains. A one-way fare from Haneda airport to Tokyo Station by limousine bus costs ¥950 and can take upwards of 55 minutes, with actual travel time depending on traffic conditions. Leave extra time for your journey, especially during peak travel times.

There are a handful of nighttime buses until 02:00, some of which stop at major train stations. If you are faced with a long wait at Haneda, consider taking one of these buses as far as a train station, and transferring to a taxi there to reduce the total cost.

Other Transport
Rental Car – Like Narita, Japan's major rental car agencies have desks at Haneda airport, but travel by car within Tokyo is not recommended. Rental car desks are located at both terminals one and two.

Taxi – Taxis run 24 hours to and from Haneda airport, making them a convenient option when the trains and buses aren't running. Taxis are the most expensive option, with a one way trip from the airport to Tokyo costing from ¥7000-11,000, depending on the traffic.

To offset the high cost, Haneda offers special taxi services. Look for taxis with 'Excellent Service' stickers on their windscreens. These taxis offer fixed fares, some manner of English language support and drivers who have been specially trained in hospitality.

A fixed-fare taxi ride from Haneda Airport to Tokyo Station area is ¥6,100, or ¥7,200 during the late-night/early morning period.

Rail to Tokyo

Tokyo is a major train hub, connected by rail to almost all of Japan (the exceptions being the islands of Okinawa).

The high-speed bullet train, the Shinkansen, links Tokyo to Japan's other major cities; it reaches maximum speeds of 320 km/h. The Tokaido line between Tokyo and Osaka was the first Shinkansen line to open, and remains the busiest today, and has carried over 5 billion passengers since it opened in 1964.

The trip between Osaka and Tokyo takes as little as 147 minutes and costs ¥14,920 (with a reserved seat) or ¥8,910 without a reserved seat. The same journey by car or bus takes 6 hours.

Traveling between Kyoto and Tokyo takes 2 hours 11 minutes and costs ¥14,370 on the Shinkansen with a reserved seat (or ¥8,360 without), compared to 5 hours 40 minutes by car. Although recent times have seen a rise in cheap domestic flights, the fact that the Shinkansen puts you directly in the Tokyo Metropolis without any need for airport transfers keeps it a competitive transport option.

Since May 2020, there have been luggage restrictions on the Tokaido - Sanyo- Kyushu Shinkansen (which includes the popular Tokyo to Osaka route). Luggage with dimensions of over 160 cm total (length + height + width) is considered oversized and requires a seat reservation with oversized storage - this can be made online or at ticket machines. This is the same price as a regular reservation. Those without reservations pay a ¥1,000 penalty. Luggage 251 cm and larger is *not* permitted aboard.

Japan Rail (JR) Pass

Foreign visitors in Japan on a tourist/sightseeing visa can look into the Japan Rail Pass. This is a ticket allowing unlimited traveling on Japan Rail (JR) Lines throughout the entire country. Japan Rail is the national rail corporation.

There are two types of JR Pass. The Ordinary Pass offers unreserved rides on any JR line (excludes some high-speed Shinkansen, but lower speed Shinkansen on the same lines may be ridden) for one week (¥29,650), two weeks (¥47,250), and three weeks (¥60,450). Reserved seats can be acquired at no extra charge.

The Green Pass is more expensive (about 30-35% extra) but allows passengers to use the green cars, the JR equivalent of a first class carriage.

The JR Rail Pass must be purchased in your home country, either online or through a licensed travel agent. The JR Rail Pass is only really cost-effective for travelers doing a lot of travel outside of Tokyo, but if you take three Shinkansen trips, the one week ticket pays for itself.

Once in Tokyo, you can use the JR Rail Pass to ride any of the JR Train lines, but be aware that travel on the subway system or private train lines is not covered by the JR Pass.

To use the JR Rail Pass, take your Exchange Order and your passport to the Japan Rail Pass counter at Narita Airport, Haneda Airport, or major stations (Tokyo Station, for example). At this time, you can specify what date you would like your Rail Pass to be valid from.

Then, when traveling, go through the manned gate at any station, showing the Rail Pass to the attendant to be allowed entry. You may also be asked to show your passport. If the station has automated ticket gates, you may also use these.

Bus to Tokyo

Japan has a network of highway buses, also known as *kousoku basu*, that connect Tokyo to the rest of the country. This is an option for travelers on a budget, as in addition to being cheaper than the Shinkansen, an overnight bus can remove the need for a hotel room.

The highway bus seats are similar to those of airplanes. Some buses have toilets on board, while others make periodic stops along the way. Most highway buses can be boarded from stops near to major train stations.

JR Highway Buses do not accept the JR Rail Pass. Tickets must be purchased through bus ticket counters at major train stations, online or over the phone (Japanese only).
The Highway Buses can be booked at kousokubus.net/JpnBus/en. To travel to Tokyo from Osaka, for example, the 8 hour 30-minute journey would set you back ¥8,000 yen for a basic fare during off-peak times (discounts apply when booking in advance).

Willer Bus has also established itself as a long-haul bus option with a good safety record.

Originally aimed at the discount market, Willer has expanded into buses with a variety of comfort upgrades, including sleep pods on selected vehicles. Willer has great English support and an excellent English website (willerexpress.com) where tickets can be purchased online, but their bus stops can be hard to locate. The main stop in Shinjuku is a long walk from the nearest train or subway station.

Fares on a Willer Bus from Osaka to Tokyo start at ¥2,900 yen for a basic seat. For women traveling alone, Willer has a policy of seating female travelers next to each other.

Transportation in Tokyo

Tokyo is well served by a public transport system that takes orderliness, safety and reliability to new heights. All of Tokyo's main tourist attractions are within walking distance of a train, subway or bus station. There are signs in English, and most train and bus stops also have English announcements.

An introduction to Tokyo's train network

Tokyo's rail and subway networks overlap and you often have several options to reach your destination. If you get stuck, ask an attendant for help. For navigation, we recommend Apple or Google Maps.

Most train and subway fares within central Tokyo range from ¥110 to ¥310. Transferring from one operator to another raises the ticket price, as does opting for a faster train. Generally speaking, of Tokyo's main rail options, the Tokyo Metro is the cheapest, followed closely by the JR Lines.

In addition to buying individual tickets or the day passes mentioned in the airport pages, there are pre-paid IC Card options that you swipe over the entry and exit gates. Both the Suica and the Pasmo travel cards can be purchased directly from either airport or any train station on arrival.

IC Cars are valid on JR East Japan trains, and many metro, buses and monorail within Tokyo (exceptions: Shinkansen, express trains, airport shuttles and highway buses - basically any train or bus that you need a seat reservation for). IC Cards give the user slightly reduced fares versus single paper tickets. The Suica card can be purchased at most JR ticket machines and is valid for 10 years after purchase. If you plan on making multiple journeys use an IC Card to avoid having to buy a ticket each time.

The Suica card costs ¥2.000 (¥1,500 pre-loaded fare plus a ¥500 deposit). If you take your Suica card to a JR station before leaving Japan, you can claim back the ¥500 deposit (minus a ¥220 handling fee) and any remaining balance on the card. The balance on your Suica card can be topped up at any JR ticket machine.

Pasmo is a pre-paid travel card that operates almost exactly like the Suica. The only difference is that the Suica is operated by JR East, and Pasmo is operated by a conglomerate of private subway and rail networks.

To purchase the Pasmo card, go to any non-JR station and look for a ticket machine with a pink Pasmo sticker on it. The Pasmo costs ¥1,000 yen, including a ¥500 balance that you can use immediately. Like the Suica, the Pasmo can be personalized with your details.

Pasmo and Suica are used interchangeably throughout Tokyo, and if purchasing a prepaid travel card, you shouldn't worry too much about which one you choose. Generally speaking, you will need to add credit to your IC Card (Suica or Pasmo) with cash; cards are not accepted.

An alternative way to use Suica is to set up a new Suica on Apple Pay. This does not require a deposit and credit can be added on your phone using a credit or debit card instead of adding it in cash at the machines.

Other rail considerations:

Train stations almost always have toilets and lockers. Most toilets have toilet paper, but some do not. It is a good idea to keep a packet of tissues on hand for these instances. There may not be hand dryers either. Adopt the Japanese habit of carrying a handkerchief in their pocket instead.

Some, but not all stations, are wheelchair accessible. If you need to use an elevator, you may have to continue down the line to a station with one, then get a taxi to your destination.

At the front and back of each train cabin is the 'priority seating area.' These are seats intended for use by the elderly, injured, pregnant women or people with small children. It is highly unlikely that a Japanese person will ask you to give up one of these seats. If you sit in one, you must be alert, and stand if you see anyone that you think needs the seat.

Using cellphones around the 'priority seating area' is banned because the phone signals have been known to interfere with people's pacemakers.

During peak hours, many trains run 'women-only' carriages, in an effort to help women avoid being groped on trains. Men must not enter these carriages between the posted times.

Station Exits

Japanese train and subway stations often have multiple exits, often very far apart from each other.

When heading towards a particular tourist attraction, there is often a recommended exit that will reduce the time needed to reach the attraction. When in the station look at the signs directing you towards the exits. Often you'll see 'For Senso-ji' or another indication of which exit to take to reach the destination.

There are also maps throughout the station building that show where local attractions are in relation to the station's exits, allowing you to orientate yourself and work out how to quickly and easily reach your destination.

When getting directions from hotel staff or tourist information centers, ask for guidance about which station exit to take. They may not always know, but if they do, it can save you a lot of time.

Map applications such as Citymapper, Google Maps and Apple Maps will also suggest the correct station exit to take.

Japan Rail (JR)

JR is Japan's national railway agency. JR has a network of train lines across Tokyo. Lines are each associated with a color, making for easy identification of trains and platforms.

Trains come in a few varieties. Local trains stop at every station, while express and limited express trains stop at certain stations only. If catching an express, check the line map to see whether or not you'll need to transfer to get to your destination - a maps/transit app will also tell you.

The **JR Chuo/Sobu Line** is worth remembering as it cuts through the center of Tokyo, linking Tokyo Station with Shinjuku, Takao, and Akihabara. Chuo Line trains are orange, while Sobu line trains are yellow.

The line travels a 35km loop around central Tokyo, hitting all the city's transport hubs and major stations. Stops on the Yamanote include Tokyo,

Ueno, Ikebukuro, Shinjuku, Shinagawa, Shibuya and Harajuku. The Yamanote line trains are a light green color.

You can purchase a ticket from an attendant at a ticket gate, although it is faster to use one of the many ticket machines around the gates. The ticket machines can display English on request.

You must select the correct fare when purchasing your ticket by using the maps above the ticket machines. If you're pressed for time, an option is to buy the cheapest ticket. When arriving at your destination station, there will be a 'fare adjustment' machine. Enter your ticket and the machine will tell you how much you owe. Enter that amount, collect your new ticket and feed it into the exit gate.

For an easier option, use an IC Card such as Suica/Pasmo and avoid having to calculate fares.

Private Railways

A number of private rail networks supplement the JR lines within Tokyo. Most connect Tokyo to commuter suburbs, while a few carry passengers to Tokyo's newer tourist destinations, for example, the Yurikamome line to Odaiba.

Travel on these private railways is not covered by the JR rail pass, but in all other respects, is like traveling on the JR network.

Tickets can be purchased at the station, or you can use your Pasmo or Suica at the ticket gate.

If purchasing tickets to a destination that includes a transfer, you can buy your ticket for both JR and private legs of the journey at your starting station.

Subway and Metro

Tokyo's trains get a lot of credit, but its subway is in many ways even more useful. Two main subway companies serve Tokyo. The Tokyo Metro, with nine lines, and the Toei (Tokyo Bureau of Transportation) Subway with four. These two subway companies have a long history of cooperation.

Passengers using day pass tickets or IC Cards can transfer between both lines, but passengers purchasing individual tickets will need to buy an additional ticket to transfer from a Metro line to a Toei line.

The subway is easy to navigate for tourists. Tickets can be purchased from ticket machines with English instructions. Each line is associated with a color, and there are lots of signs and announcements in English.

What can be confusing is how many exits each station has but there are frequent maps, and, at tourist destinations, signs directing you to the exit closest to the sights. As well as paying individual fares in cash or IC cards, the subways offer a range of passes for people using their lines.

Tokyo Subway Ticket: The Tokyo Subway Ticket is valid for a pre-selected period on all Tokyo Metro and Toei lines, starting from the ticket's first use.

The Tokyo Subway Ticket can only be purchased by visitors on a tourist visa. You can buy from selected travel agents and some hotels (see www.tokyometro.jp).

Pricing is ¥800 for 24 hours, ¥1,200 for 48 hours and ¥1,500 for 72 hours. Child tickets are half price.

Tokyo Metro Ticket: The Tokyo Metro 24 hour ticket costs ¥600 (¥300 for kids), and gives unlimited rides on the Tokyo Metro. It is valid for 24 hours from the moment of first use. The ticket becomes invalid if not used on the day of purchase.

Common One Day Pass:
The Common One Day pass gives 24 hours unlimited travel on both Tokyo Metro and Toei Subway lines. It costs ¥900 (¥450 for kids).

Tokyo Combination Ticket:
The Tokyo Combination Ticket gives 24 hours travel on the Tokyo Metro, Toei . Subway, Toei Streetcar, Toei Bus (except buses with reserved seats), all sections of Nippori-Toneri Liner and all JR lines within the Tokyo metropolitan area. It costs ¥1,600 (¥800 for kids), and can only be purchased up to one month in advance.

Bus

Tokyo is served by several bus companies. Rides within Tokyo have a flat-rate fare of ¥210, with a few exceptions—see below.

Unlike most buses in Japan, you board at the front of the bus and you pay your fare then. You can pay your fare in coins or notes or by IC Card. If using an IC Card on a Toei bus, you'll receive a ¥100 discount on your next bus ride, providing it is within 90 minutes of your initial ride.

Edo Bus is a community bus run by the Chuo ward office, serving destinations within Central Tokyo. A ticket is ¥100, but a one day pass of ¥300 allows unlimited use of the Edo buses. Pasmo and Suica can also be used (see city.chuo.lg.jp for a map).

The Sumida-ku Loop Buses cover the Sumida district. They have glass ceilings and are popular with Japanese sightseers, visiting more obscure tourist destinations, but cover a variety of locations. The Northwest route stops at the house of novelist Mori Ogai, and Shirahige-jimja, a shrine immortalized in the ukiyo-e (Edo-period woodcuts) of Katsuhika Hokusai (Hokusai's painted the iconic

picture of Mt. Fuji framed by waves).

The Northeast route includes several small temples and Taisho Minka-en, an old Japanese style house now open to the public. The Southern route connects with the water bus, and includes more popular destinations, such as the Edo-Tokyo Museum and the Hokusai Museum. A single fare is ¥100, but a day pass for all three routes is ¥300. All three routes converge on Oshiage station, location of the Tokyo Skytree.

Buses are less frequent and take longer than the trains. It can also be hard to locate the bus stops, and there is very little English signage. It is better to look up the bus you want and your stop in advance. Check with tourist information at the closest big train station or look online. Google Maps, Citymapper and Apple Maps can solve most of these issues.

The buses are identified by a Kanji character associated with their route and a number and can be hard to identify.

Stops are announced by an electronic recording in Japanese ahead of time, although English announcements are increasingly common. When your stop is approaching, press the button as Japanese buses don't stop at every stop.

Like trains, Japanese buses have priority seating reserved for elderly, sick and pregnant travelers. Be mindful of other passengers and prepared to give up your seat if necessary. Unlike highway buses, city buses do not have room for luggage, so travel light.

Taxi and Uber

Taxis:
Tokyo taxis are more expensive than trains and buses, with a starting fare of ¥730, increasing ¥320 for every 1km, or ¥51 every minute in traffic. They also have a 20% surcharge between 22:00-05:00.

However, since Tokyo's trains and subway stops running at 01:00, taxis are a good option if you are out late, particularly if you're part of a group.

Rear taxi doors are opened by the driver. Signal for a ride and the driver will open the door for you.

In preparation for the Olympics, most taxi companies are rolling out English support. Even so, if you are going to a more unusual destination, it might be a good idea to come prepared with a map, or the address written in Japanese.

Uber:
The government ruled that ride-sharing is illegal and so

Uber has survived in Tokyo by becoming a taxi-hailing service. This allows you to be cashless in a city that unusually requires cash for almost everything.

Driving

Tokyo's fast and convenient public transport makes Tokyo accessible to all. If you decide to drive, you're contending with crowded roads, busy traffic and a difficult navigation system. Invest in a good GPS system, or if renting a car, ask the rental agency to demonstrate its use.

Cars drive on the left, and speeds range from between 30-40km/h on Tokyo's crowded residential streets, 50-60km/h on the city limits, and up to 100km/h on the highway.

Japan has a zero-tolerance approach to drunk driving. Don't risk it. Instead, many

taxis offer a service where they will drive you home in your car with a second taxi following to retrieve your driver.

Free parking in Tokyo is extremely rare. Parking is strictly regulated, and parking outside designated parking zones or in a reserved parking space, can see your car towed and you fined.

Parking lots often feature barriers. Once your car is parked in a space, the barrier raises, trapping your car until you pay the fee and retrieve your vehicle.

There are two types of gas

station in Tokyo. 'Full' stands for 'full-service.' As you pull into the station, an attendant will direct you to park at a pump, enquire what you require (*manten* means 'full tank'), and then fill your car. You'll be asked whether you're paying in cash (*genkin*) or by credit card (*kado*). 'Self' indicates a self-service gas station.

Water Buses

Tokyo's network of water buses is less an effective transport system, and more of a tourist service, but they are still a fun way to see the city. The leisurely pace of the boats makes a nice

change from the trains, and there is a guided commentary track in English and Japanese. Waterbuses depart from piers in Hinode, Asakusa, Hamarikyu, Toyosu, Odaiba Seaside

Park, Palette Town and Tokyo Big Sight. Fares vary according to distance.

Water buses do not run in bad weather and be canceled at short notice.

Cycling

Cycling in Tokyo can be unnerving! But if you can brave heavy traffic and a lack of bicycle lanes, cycling has a lot of advantages, freeing you from the constraints of train and bus timetables and allowing you to explore Tokyo at your leisure. Don't be alarmed if you hear a lot of horns. In Japan, cars honk to thank other drivers or to warn cyclists that they are approaching.

Cyclists are supposed to ride on the left side road, but you will often see people riding on the footpath if they are not inconveniencing pedestrians. Helmets are optional, but if cycling after dark, lights and reflective gear are required by law.

Cycling while drunk, listening to headphones, using a cellphone, or holding an umbrella are all against the law. It is also illegal to ride side by side with another cyclist. After umbrellas, bicycles are the single most likely item to be stolen in Japan. Be careful to park your cycle in an approved cycle zone. It is common to see Japanese cyclists leaving their bikes in clear defiance of signs indicating no-bicycle parking zones, but don't be tempted to follow their example.

Periodically, ward officers come along with trucks and remove any violating bicycles, and you will have to pay a hefty fine before the bike is returned.

You can take bikes onto trains at no extra cost, providing that the bike is broken down and placed in a special bicycle bag called 'rinko bukuro'.

Rental cycles are available throughout Tokyo, and are even offered by some hotels. If you want a helmet, go to a dedicated rental cycle shop and ask to rent one with your bike. If you love cycling, but want some guidance before you tackle Tokyo, there are a number of companies offering cycling tours of Tokyo. Tokyo Great Cycling Tour claims to be the first, and has 15 years of experience guiding cyclists through Tokyo.

A cycle tour through Chuo-ku, taking in Nihombashi, Ningyo-cho, the sumo district of Ryogoku, Asakusa, Ueno Park and the Imperial Palace gardens, lasting 6 hours costs ¥12,000 and includes the cost of your bike rental, lunch and a bottle of water (see tokyocycling.jp).

Neighborhood Guides

Tokyo is composed of 23 special wards, which act as individual cities - of little help to the tourist wanting to explore the city!

We've singled out areas of particular interest to tourists and grouped them by location.

Central Tokyo - The three central wards, Chiyoda, Chuo and Minato, comprise the old core of Tokyo, where business and political power was centered.

Modern Tokyo - As the city expanded, sub-centers were formed to meet the needs of the population. Shinjuku is now the current center of government, while Shibuya is a trendy shopping district and fashion hotspot. Shinagawa is a transport hub, while Rinkai, comprising the island of Odaiba, offers a gateway to Japan's future.

Old Tokyo - Some of the atmosphere of Edo-Period Tokyo still remains in Tokyo's older suburbs. Ueno and Asakusa's temples and shopping streets bustle with visitors, while sumo stables in Sumida still operate on much the same lines as they did centuries ago.

Further Afield - Finally, take advantage of Japan's excellent public transport to explore further afield. You are spoiled for choice. The beautiful Fuji Five Lakes, volcanic hotspot Hakone, former capital Kamakura, and peaceful Nikko are all easy day trips from Tokyo.

ATTRACTION KEY:
Throughout this guide, we include a grid with each listing with helpful information. The key below is a guide to what each symbol means.

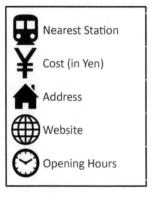

Nearest Station

Cost (in Yen)

Address

Website

Opening Hours

Reading this section thoroughly will enable you to create an itinerary to suit your individual interests while avoiding long hours traveling between attractions. Dining options and accommodation are listed to enable you to base yourself conveniently close to where you want to spend your time.

As will become apparent as you read this guide, there are a wealth of things to do, including many with no admission charge.

Admission prices stated are 'on-the-door' rates, and cheaper tickets are often available by booking in advance online, or from other sources.

Museums and galleries that are listed as providing free admission are completely free of charge, without the need to obtain a ticket. However, a donation on the way out, or a small purchase from the gift shop is appreciated.

Remember that popular locations may have long waits to get in during busier periods of the year.

Many attractions have variable opening times depending on the day of the week, the month of the year, and whether it is term time or school holidays. To avoid disappointment, we recommend you check the opening times and dates with each attraction prior to your visit.

Tokyo has a variety of rail and subway networks, and many attractions are served by multiple stations. Where applicable, multiple stations have been listed.

Central Tokyo: Chiyoda

With Edo-Castle at its heart, Chiyoda was once the cultural, political and business center of Tokyo. As Imperial influence declined, so did the district, especially when the houses of government moved to Shinjuku in 1990. In recent years, Chiyoda has seen an intense revival.

The Marunouchi area around Tokyo station is an exciting showcase of the best of modern Tokyo, blending cutting edge architecture with beautiful restorations of iconic Tokyo buildings.

Chiyoda's wide umbrella includes Electronic hotspot Akihabara, as well as the book capital of Japan, Jimbocho, and numerous shrines and temples.

Chiyoda is a place to explore at leisure, dipping in and out of its museums, stores and cafés.

See and Do

Imperial Palace Grounds and Garden

 JR and Tokyo Metro: Tokyo Station (10-15 mins)

¥ Free

 〒100-8111 東京都千代田区千代田1-1 (1-1 Chiyoda, Chiyoda-ku, Tokyo, Japan 100-8111)

sankan.kunaicho.go.jp/english/guide/koukyo.html

East Gardens 09:00-16:30, Outer Gardens always open.

The Imperial Palace started life as Edo Castle, built in 1457 by Ota Dokan.

During the Edo period, the castle was the shogun's residence and the seat of military and political power. Today all that remains of the Edo-period castle are the defense walls, the moat and a scattering of buildings that survived military upheaval, fires, earthquakes and the ravages of WWII.

The Imperial family still dwells in the palace on the castle grounds, but the building is not open to the public. Visitors can access the Inner Garden through reserving a spot on one of two daily 75 minute tours by contacting the Imperial Household Agency.

The East Garden and Outer Gardens are open to the public year-round, however. The East Garden is administered by the Imperial Household Agency and contains a garden in Edo-period style as well as *Musashino copse*, a forest that was transplanted to the Imperial gardens to save it from being demolished.

The Imperial Palace Outer Gardens have many attractions, including a 5k jogging trail with plenty of amenities that encircles the palace.

There are many picturesque spots along the route, such as Nijubashi, a double-bridge dating from 1886, and Fushimi-yagura, a small keep moved to Edo-castle from Fushimi-castle in Kyoto.

Kitte

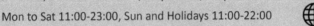

🚇 JR: Tokyo Station
Tokyo Metro: Tokyo Station or Nijubashimae Station
Toei Subway: Otemachi Station

¥ Free

🏠 〒100-7090 東京都千代田区丸の内 2-7-2
JP Tower, 2-7-2 Marunouchi, Chiyoda-ku, Tokyo Postcode: 100-7090

🕐 Mon to Sat 11:00-23:00, Sun and Holidays 11:00-22:00

🌐 jptower-kitte.jp

Kitte is a shopping mall complex housed in the former Tokyo Central Post Office. The redevelopers kept the frontage of the five-story low-rise of the original 1933 Post Office building, while expanding upwards in the sleek and modern Japan Post Tower,

38 floors of offices, restaurants and retail.

Inside, the ground floor is still used as a post office. The second and third floors have been turned into the Intermediatheque with the collaboration of Tokyo University. The Intermediatheque has

venues for public seminars and workshops and a museum of academic culture with exhibits.

Kitte has restaurants and high-end fashion, accessories and cafés. You can do all your gift shopping and mail it home without leaving the building.

Chidorigafuchi Moat

🚇 Toei Subway and Tokyo Metro: Kudanshita Station

¥ Boats: ¥800 for 30 mins in sakura season, ¥500 for 30 mins at other times.

🏠 〒102-0083 東京千代田区北の丸公園−1 (Kitanomarukoen-1, Chiyoda-ku, Tokyo Postcode: 102-0083)

🕐 Check locally

If you're in Tokyo during spring, you can't miss Chidorigafuchi, the best cherry-blossom viewing location in Tokyo.

Chidorigafuchi is one of the twelve moats surrounding the Imperial Palace. Approximately 260 cherry trees are planted either side of the moat. You can step through the charming Tayasu-mon Gate and follow the 700m walkway on foot, but the best way to enjoy

Chidorigafuchi's blossoms is by boat.

You can rent a boat (capacity 2 adults and 1 child) from a boathouse beside the moat. Although the boats are available year-round except in winter, they're only in high demand during the cherry blossom season.

If visiting during cherry blossom season, allow plenty of time— it can take

up two to four hours to get a boat. Fortunately, the cherry trees are illuminated after dark.

If you want to combine sakura viewing with a picnic, continue walking to Kitano Park where the cherry blossoms continue.

At other times of the year, consider visiting Chidorigafuchi Cemetery, a simple graveyard for the unidentified dead of WWII.

Tokyo Station and Marunouchi

  Tokyo Station

 ¥ Free

 〒100-0005 東京都千代田区丸の内1-9-1 (1-9-1 Marunouchi, Chiyoda, Tokyo, Postcode: 100-0005)

tokyostationcity.com/en/

Shopping: 10:00-22:00, Marunouchi: 11:00-23:00

There is no better representation of Tokyo's endless ability to reinvent itself, than Tokyo Station.

On the Marunouchi gate side, the station has been beautifully restored to its 1914 red-brick facade. Within the station, domed entrances and marble floors make you feel as if you are entering a palace rather than a train station - until you spot the ticket barriers.

On the other side of Tokyo station, the Yaesu entrance is a modern construction of glass and steel. Within and beneath Tokyo Station are a variety of upmarket shopping complexes.

On both sides of Tokyo Station are gleaming skyscrapers. Many offer views over Tokyo station from their dining floors.

Marunouchi Oazu houses the Maruzen bookstore which has a fabulous selection of English language books, magazines and newspapers, including a great collection of English books on Japanese history, culture and literature. The top floor of the bookstore has an amazing selection of stationery.

Tokyo International Forum

 JR and Tokyo Metro: Yurakucho Station.

 ¥ N/A

 〒100-0005 東京都千代田区丸の内 3-5-1
3-5-1 Marunouchi, Chiyoda, Tokyo Postcode: 100-0005

 07:00-22:00

 t-i-forum.co.jp/en

Tokyo International Forum lives up to its name, being both Tokyo's largest convention center, with one hall alone seating 5000 people, and decorated with the work of artists from Japan and around the world.

The distinctive glass and steel building was designed by Uruguay architect Rafael Vinoly, in the shape of an eleven floor high boat.

Inside, the ambient natural light and air of the lobby create a natural meeting place, and cafés and restaurants invite people to linger. An underground walkway links the lobby to the large auditorium wing.

The Tokyo International Forum houses seven halls, and an exhibition space. It houses the Mitsuo Aida Museum celebrating the life and art of the calligrapher.

Among the hundreds of events hosted annually are musicals, concerts, and antique fairs—the Oedo Antique Market takes place on the first and third Sunday of the month in the plaza.

Kanda Jimbocho Bookstore District

 Tokyo Metro and Toei Subway: Jimbocho Station
JR: Suidobashi Station

 東京千代田区神田神保町
Jinbocho, Kanda, Chiyoda-ku, Tokyo

Bookstores are typically open 10:00-18:30 and many close on Sundays and public holidays.

¥ Free

 kitazawa.co.jp is one seller.

Jimbocho's association with books started in 1913 with a single bookstore, opened by a University professor. A century later, that bookstore is now a publishing house (Iwanami Shoten), and Jimbocho is Tokyo's book capital. With over 170 new and used bookstores in the area, Jimbocho is a must for book lovers.

Most of Jimbocho's book stores are located on south-facing Yasukuni-dori, to protect the books from exposure.

You can find anything from used and rare books, to pulp fiction in bargain bins outside the stores. Most of the books are in Japanese with the occasional English book thrown in. Stores notable for the range of English books are Kitazawa Bookstore, the Isseido Booksellers, and Books Sanseido.

Jimbocho has serious literary credentials. Not only is the district within walking distance of three Universities (students were

the first patrons of the bookstores and have kept the district humming over the years), but it is also the haunt of Haruki Murakami. Murakami once operated a jazz club in the area, and Jimbocho makes numerous appearances in his writing.

Giant manga publisher Shueisha also has headquarters in Jimbocho, as do many literary societies, including the Tokyo Book Binding and Literature Preservation Society.

Tokyo Daijingu Shrine

 JR, Tokyo Metro and Toei Subway: Iidabashi Station (7 mins)

 〒102-0071 富士見千代田区２−４−１
2-4-1 Fujimi, Chiyoda-ku, Tokyo Postcode: 102-0071

 Sunrise to Sunset

 ¥ Free. Donations welcomed.

tokyodaijingu.or.jp

Tokyo Daijingu's claim to fame is that it founded the Shinto marriage ceremony, now widely performed throughout Japan. It has a reputation for bringing about successful marriages and so it attracts visitors wishing to improve their romantic prospects.

On weekends, the shrine becomes so popular that visitors are divided into two lines. If you are after a love charm, get into the right line - it is believed to be more powerful.

Tokyo Daijingu is one of the five major shrines of Tokyo, and one of three in Chiyoda.

Tokyo Daijingu, which roughly translates as Great Tokyo Shrine, is also known as O-Ise-sama, because it enshrines three deities associated with Ise Jingu, one of the main Shinto sites.

Those deities include the sun goddess, Amaterasu-Sume-Ohkami, from whom the Imperial family is believed to have descended.

Ise-Jingu, located in Mie prefecture, was a popular pilgrimage destination in the Edo-period, but the difficulty of traveling at that time made it hard for ordinary people to make the journey. In 1880, Emperor Meiji approved the building of a new temple for Ise-Jingu's gods in Tokyo. After the Kanto earthquake, the shrine was moved to its current location.

Mitsubishi Ichigokan Museum

 Tokyo Station

 Varies by event.

〒100-0005 東京都千代田区丸の内 2–6-2 (2-6-2 Marunouchi, Chiyoda-ku, Tokyo Postcode:100-0005)

mimt.jp/english/

🕙 10:00-18:00

The Mitsubishi Ichigokan Museum is another example of Marunouchi revitalizing Tokyo's past. The original Mitsubishi Ichigokan building occupied the site from 1894-1968. One of the first Western buildings in Japan, the Japanese government invited English architect Josiah Conder to design it.

The current building is a loving recreation that used the original plans and some of the same building materials. The result is a gorgeous building as worthy of notice as the collections of art it houses.

The gallery houses Western Art of the 19th century, in particular over 200 hundred works of the artist Henri Toulouse-Lautrec. It collects art and objects dating between 1880-1890, the period in which the Ichigokan was originally designed and built. Of special interest is the Japonisme collection, books of the prints that first introduced Japanese art to Europe.

The museum also contains a lovely English garden in the Queen Anne style. The many outdoor seats make it a pleasant place to stop and rest. Cafe 1894 provides refreshments in a charming setting.

Akihabara

 JR: Akihabara Station
Tokyo Metro: Suehirocho Station
Toei Subway: Iwamoto Station

 東京都千代田区神田花岡町 (Kanda Hanaokachō, Chiyoda-ku, Tokyo)

e-akihabara.jp

🕙 Most big shops: 10:00-21:00

Akihabara earned its nickname 'Electric Town' in the 1930s, when the area became a hotspot for entrepreneurs dealing in household electronics.

In the 1980s, the focus shifted to computers, attracting a new type of customer base. Akihabara became the base for numerous electronics shops but also where they launched new products.

Today, Akihabara caters to geek culture with an array of video game, comic and animation stores and goods on offer alongside cutting edge electronics.

The main draw for foreign tourists is the electronic shops where there is still a chance of picking up a bargain on the latest cameras and computers.

Just be warned that much of these goods are intended for the Japanese market and English support may be limited. If you decide that the tax-free discount is worth it, head to the huge electronic department stores such as Laox, Yamada Denki, Yodobashi Camera, Sofmap and Akky.

If you're keen to experience Japanese pop culture, then the Tokyo Anime Center on the 4th floor of the UDX building has exhibitions and souvenirs.

Depending on your tastes, a visit to a maid-cafe can either be extremely creepy or a way to experience otaku culture.

Super Potato, Mandarake, Animate and Gamers sell anime-goods, comics and games, though few of these will be available in English!

Kanda Myojin

 JR and Tokyo Metro: Ochanomizu Station (5 mins)

 Free. Donations accepted.

 〒101-0021 東京都千代田区外神田2－16－2 (2-16-2 Sotokanda, Chiyoda-ku, Tokyo, Postcode: 101-0021

 kandamyoujin.or.jp

 Always open.

When Akihabara decided to cater for the computing crowd, the local shrine, Kanda Myojin, followed suit. The shrine sells charms that mimic computer hardware designed to protect electronic devices from harm.

Tokugawa Ieyasu (the first of the Tokugawa shogunate) once paid his respects here. Now the shrine attracts technophiles wanting the shrine's protection on their newly purchased gadgets.

Kanda Myojin Shrine dates from 730 AD, but like most of Tokyo's temples, it was destroyed and rebuilt multiple times. The current building was finished in 1934.

The shrine is dedicated to Daikoku and Ebisu, gods of wealth and luck respectively. Business owners have been coming to the shrine for centuries to secure the blessing of the deity on their store. A small step from there to computing!

Kanda Myojin is also the focal point of the Kanda festival, one of Japan's top three festivals. Thousands of people carrying portable shrines throng the streets surrounding the shrine. The festival is held mid-May on odd-numbered years only (in even-numbered years, the Sanno festival is held).

Dating back to the Edo-period, the Kanda festival started as a celebration of the shogun's rule, and was one of only two festivals allowed within the grounds of Edo castle. The other was the Sanno festival.

Competition between the two festivals grew so fierce that eventually it was ruled that they would take place bi-annually, avoiding any clashes.

National Diet Building

 Tokyo Metro:
Nagatacho Station

¥ Free

 〒100-0014 永田町
千代田区1－7－1
(1-7-1 Nagatacho,
Chiyoda, Tokyo
Postcode: 100-0014)

 sangiin.go.jp

🕐 Tours: Mon
(2:00pm), Tues-Fri
(3:00pm)

The National Diet Building is Japan's political center, the place where the diet assembles to hold sessions. The House of Representatives meet in the left wing, the House of Councillors debate in the right wing. Anyone can visit the Diet on a weekday, except for when a plenary session is meeting.

Tours of the Diet Building take roughly an hour and are conducted by Diet guards. You must check in at the reception desk prior to the tour. Look for the signboard reading 'Tours of the House of Councillors: Entrance.' The Tour includes the public gallery, Emperor's room, and Central Hall, among other places.

For more detailed information, follow the instructions on the official page: http://bit.ly/diettours.

Hibiya Park

 Tokyo Metro: Hibiya station
JR: Yurakucho station (8 mins)

🏠 〒100-0012 千代田区日比谷公園 1－6
1-6 Hibiiya-koen, Chiyoda-ku Postcode: 100-0012

🕐 Always open

¥ Free

🌐 tokyo-park.or.jp

Hibiya Park is a delightful Western-style park dotted with sculptures donated by foreign governments and Edwardian-era neo-gothic monuments. The park's location south of the Imperial Gardens means it is often missed by tourists. However, because Hibiya park is not as crowded, it makes a great place to relax after a day shopping or sightseeing.

Hibiya Park has an interesting history. The former military parade grounds opened to the public in 1903 as one of Japan's first Western-style parks. Two years later, it was the site of riots that killed 17 people and ushered in Japan nationalism.

During WWII, the park's trees were used as timber, while the park's fences were melted down to make war supplies. Post-war restoration culminated in 1961 with the addition of the park's magnificent fountain.

Today, Hibiya Park is well known for its concerts and its rose and tulip gardens. If you drop by at the weekend, it's likely you'll encounter some form of concert or festival.

Throughout the year it hosts events, including Oktoberfest (in mid-September), and the Tokyo Christmas Market. Hibiya Park is the endpoint for the Tokyo marathon.

Hie Shrine

 Tokyo Metro: Akasaka-mitsuke Station (5 mins)

 Free. Donations accepted.

 〒100-0014 千代田区永田町２－１０－５ (2-10-5 Nagatacho, Chiyoda, Tokyo, Postcode: 100-0014)

 hiejinja.net

 April-Sep: 05:00-18:00, Oct-March: 6:00-17:00

If you want to experience rows upon rows of red *torii* gates but can't make it to Kyoto's Fushimi Inari Taisha, head to downtown Hie shrine.

Situated at the top of a steep hill, the shrine is approached by climbing through *torii* (archways) so dense they form a tunnel. If you're exhausted after sight-seeing, no problem. The shrine also has an escalator.

Hie Shrine is linked to the Tokugawa shogunate, with the Tokugawa shoguns enshrined here. Tokugawa Ieyasu worshipped the god of Hie Shrine as the protector of Edo, relocating the shrine within the castle grounds for his family's personal use.

Since 1604, when his son Tokugawa Hidetada moved the shrine to its present location, the shrine has been popular with the people of Tokyo.

Today, Hie Shrine safeguards many treasures, including the sword *Itomaki-no-tachi,* one of Japan's national treasures.

The National Museum of Modern Art, Tokyo

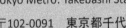

 Tokyo Metro: Takebashi Station

 500 yen (general admission only)

 〒102-0091　東京都千代田区北の丸公園1-1
1-1 Kitanomaru Koen, Chiyoda-ku, Postcode:102-0091

 10:00-17:00 (10:00-20:00 on Sat and Fridays). Closed Mon. Open on holiday Mondays and closed on the next day.

 momat.go.jp

The National Museum of Modern Art, Tokyo, is Japan's first National Art Museum. It opened in 1952 with the mission of heightening public appreciation of contemporary art. Sixty-five years later, MOMAT's collection offers visitors a crash course in modern Japanese art.

The highlights of the Modern Art collection include the works of Japanese modernist Ryusei Kishida, and around 8000 ukiyo-e (Japanese woodcuts) that had been scattered abroad.

The building itself classifies as a piece of art, designed by Yoshiro Taniguchi. It houses a library, restaurant and museum shop in addition to the galleries.

The Crafts Gallery opened 1977 to showcase modern crafts, including traditional crafts such as lacquerware, woodwork and ceramics, to graphic design, industrial design and textiles.

The Gallery is housed in the former headquarters of the Imperial Guard. This 1910 redbrick building fell into disrepair and was intended to be demolished. Recognizing its importance as an example of Meiji-period architecture, the building was saved and converted into a gallery.

Holy Resurrection Cathedral

 Tokyo Metro and JR: Ochanomizu Station

 300 yen

 〒101-0062　東京都千代田区神田駿河台4-1-3 (4-1-3 Kanda-Surugadai, Chiyoda-ku, Postcode: 101-0062)

 nikolaido.org

April-Sep: 13:00-16:00, Oct-March: 13:00-15:30

The Holy Resurrection Cathedral is a Byzantine style cathedral and the headquarters of the Orthodox Church of Japan.

The Cathedral is affectionately nicknamed Nikolai-do after the Archbishop Ivan Dmitrievich Kasatkin, later St. Nicholas of Japan, who oversaw the cathedral's design, construction and founded the Orthodox church in Japan.

Kasatkin toured his home-country Russia to raise funds to build the cathedral. He devoted his life to improving Japanese-Russian relations throughout the Meiji period, culminating in the Holy Resurrection Cathedral's construction.

When it was first constructed, the Cathedral looked down on the Imperial Palace. When the building was finished in 1891, its unusual and romantic Byzantine style made a big impact on contemporary Tokyo with the cathedral often appearing in contemporary art and literature.

During the Great Kanto Earthquake, the Cathedral was significantly damaged. The bell tower and dome collapsed and had to be reconstructed. The current building is less ornate and slightly smaller than the original but still striking.

Eat

Ninja Akasaka
Nearest Station: Tokyo Metro: Akasaka-mitsuke Stn
Phone: 03-5157-3936
Address: 〒100-0014 東京都千代田区永田町 2-14-3 赤坂東急プラザ1 F (Akasaka Tokyu Plaza 1F, 2-14-3 Nagata-cho, Chiyoda-ku, Tokyo Postcode: 100-0014)
Hours: 17:30-1:00 (doors close 22:30)
Website: ninjaakasaka.com

Japanese fusion food as you have never seen it before, Ninja Akasaka isn't a restaurant—it's an experience.

From the moment you arrive in the nearly pitch-black lobby to have your reservation checked by a ninja, you know you're in for an experience. Ninja Akasaka is an over the top dining experience that combines illusions and magic tricks with genuinely good food.

The chef combines high-quality ingredients in a variety of dishes, using the best of Japanese and European techniques to build a fun, yet flavorful menu. Ideal for birthdays or special celebrations. ¥10,000 for 8-course set menu; ¥7,000 for 6 courses.

Ramen Street
Nearest Station: Tokyo Stn
Phone: 03-3211-0055
Address: 東京駅一番街 B1 東京ラーメンストリート内 1 - 9 - 1 丸の内, 千代田区 (Tokyo Station Ichibangai Ramen Street, 1-9-1 Marunouchi, Chiyoda-ku Postcode 100-0005)
Hours: 07:30-23:00
Website: rokurinsha.com

To sample the best ramen in Japan, you don't have to leave Tokyo Station. The country's eight best ramen stores were invited to open branches within Tokyo Station, near the Yaesu exit known as Ramen Street.

Ramen varies widely from region to region within Japan. Which style you prefer will come down to individual taste, but the most popular is Rokurinsha (details above). Ramen starts at ¥830 and goes up to ¥1,060.

At peak lunch hours, the queue to enter Rokurinsha can be as long as 30 minutes to 1 hour.

Fairycake Fair
Nearest Station: Tokyo Stn
Phone: 03-3211-0055
Address: 〒100-0005 本 東京駅 構内 B1 グランスタ
GRANSTA (Tokyo Station B1F, 1-9-1 Marunouchi, Chiyoda-ku, Tokyo Postcode: 100-0005)
Hours: 08:00-22:00 (Sundays, hols 08:00-21:00)

Website: fairycake.jp

Fairycake Fair is a bakery located in the Tokyo Station GRANSTA mall. It is mostly known for its traditional English style cupcakes, but it is their impeccable decoration that sets them apart.

Choose between those decorated as cute animals, standard (strawberry shortcake and classic mont-blanc), or seasonal. Cupcakes are sold individually (around ¥500), or in boxes of 4, 6, or 9.

Yurakucho's Gado-shita
Nearest Station: JR, Tokyo Metro: Yurakucho Stn
Phone: 03-6252-5500
Address: 〒100-0006 東京都千代田区有楽町2-3-5 aune 有楽町3F (aune Yurakucho 3F, 2-3-5, Yuurakucho, Chiyoda-ku, Tokyo, Postcode: 100-0006)
Hours: 17:00 to 23:30
Website: akuzo-yurakucho.com

The Gado-shita is a lively

restaurant district built directly below the tracks of the Yamanote line. The restaurants spread almost to Tokyo Station in the Marunouchi district.

There are a few European restaurants, but the majority are *izakaya*—Japanese-style pubs—and *yakitori* (grilled chicken on skewers) restaurants.

If you want to be assured of Wi-Fi and an English menu, then try *Rakuzouutage* (details above). In addition to the usual izakaya fare, there is an all you can drink menu. The average price for dinner is about ¥3,500.

Stay

Sakura Hotel Jimbocho
Nearest Station: Jimbocho
Phone: 03-3261-3939
Address: 〒101-0051 東京都千代田区神田神保町2-21-4 (2-21-4 Kanda-Jimbocho, Chiyoda-ku, Tokyo Postcode: 101-0051)
Website: sakura-hotel.co.jp/jimbocho

The 2-star Sakura Hotel combines hotel and hostel to provide a place to stay conveniently close to Tokyo's major attractions that won't break the bank.

There are a male-dormitory

and a female-dormitory in the basement for ¥3,300 per night, and then simple single rooms starting at ¥6,300. If you have a group, consider the group rooms, able to accommodate 3-5 people.

There is a 24-hour cafe and bar on the first floor with a cheap breakfast set.

Tokyo Station Hotel
Nearest Station: Tokyo Stn
Phone: 03-5220-1111
Address: 〒100-0005 東京都千代田区丸の内1-9-1 (1-9-1 Marunouchi, Chiyoda, Tokyo, Postcode: 100-0005)

Website: thetokyostationhotel.jp

Tokyo Station is the ultimate in locations. Located within the iconic 100-year-old station building, the 5-star hotel combines an appreciation for the building's heritage with luxurious contemporary accommodation for guests.

Breakfast is served in a beautifully airy atrium, while guests who opt for the high-end luxury suites can stay within the Station building itself.

Central: Chuo (Ginza, Tsukiji)

Chuo means 'Central,' and historically was the commercial center of Tokyo. Today, Chuo shares that title with Shinjuku, but a large proportion of Japan's business still takes place here.

Chuo is home to the glitzy and upmarket Ginza district, named for a silver mint that used to exist in the district, as well as Tsukiji, home to Japan's most famous market.

Chuo is also the location of Nihombashi, the bridge that was the gateway into Tokyo during the Edo-period. A thriving marketplace grew up around the bridge, including the original Tsukiji fish market, which still exists in the district today. Nihonbashi was also where the wholesale business of the Mitsui family was located, which became Japan's first department store—Mitsukoshi.

The department store continues to thrive in Ginza, and the collection of stores with the high-end fashion and brand stores are an attraction in themselves.

See and Do
Ginza Mitsukoshi

 Tokyo Metro: Ginza Station

 Free

 104-8212 東京都中央区銀座4-6-16
4-6-16, Ginza, Chuo-ku, Tokyo Postcode: 104-8212

 10:00-20:00

 mitsukoshi.mistore.jp

Ginza Mitsukoshi is Japan's oldest surviving department store.

Founded in 1673 by the Mitsui family, Mistukoshi is now an internationally known brand. Ginza Mitsukoshi is the original and flagship. The bronze lion outside the main entrance is an icon and a popular meeting point.

Inside, the store retains the luxury and glitz of a time passed, down to gloved doormen. If you arrive for the doors opening, you can enjoy the entire staff assembling to greet customers with a bow.

Mitsukoshi showcases the best of Japan's fashion, luxury goods and traditional artwork.

There are services for foreign visitors, including a service counter near the entrance with English speakers, and a tourist information office in the basement where tourists can exchange money and receive information about tax-free shopping. There's also a duty-free store on the 8th floor.

One of the highlights of the department store is the basement where the food is - with samples!

For a true taste of Tokyo, grab a *bento*, a Japanese style lunch box, and head to nearby Hama-rikyu for a picnic.

Kabuki-za

 Tokyo Metro: Higashi-Ginza Station

 Single-act: ¥800-2000, All: ¥4000-21,000

 〒104-0061 東京都中央区銀座4-12-15 (4-12-15 Ginza, Chuo-ku, Tokyo Postcode: 104-0061)

 kabuki-za.co.jp

Typical hours: 10:00am-9:00pm (matinee: 11:00, evening: 16:30)

Kabuki is the most accessible of Japan's traditional theater forms.

Unlike *Noh* dramas, *Kabuki* developed to entertain the common people. Its hallmarks are exuberant and gaudy performances, with over the top costumes and make-up paired with equally exaggerated and codified gestures. It's the equivalent of British pantomime.

Despite this, the language used is so archaic, most Japanese people struggle to understand it. All parts, even the female characters, are played by men, and the actors are accompanied by traditional Japanese instruments.

There is no better place to take in a *Kabuki* performance than Kabuki-za.

A typical performance at the Kabuki-za consists of three to four acts showcasing scenes from a variety of famous dramas, and lasts for about four hours with the chance to buy boxed meals in the long intervals between the acts. If you're on a schedule, relax! You can opt to watch one of the acts instead.

The front seats are kept for customers who stay for the entire performance, but 90 sitting and 60 standing tickets are sold for each act. Tickets are sold on the day, so get in quickly.

You can also rent a headset with an English guide to help decipher the show.

Bank of Japan Currency Museum

 Tokyo Metro: Mitsukoshimae Station
JR: Tokyo Station (8 mins)

 〒103-0021 東京都中央区日本橋本石町1-3-1
1-3-1 Nihonbashi Hongokucho, Chuo-ku, Tokyo Postcode: 103-0021

 9:30-16:30 (Entry closes at 16:00), closed Mondays and National Holidays. Open when Mon is a national holiday.

¥ Free

 imes.boj.or.jp

The Ginza district has a long association with money, making it the perfect place for the Bank of Japan Currency Museum.

The suburb's name comes from a former silver mint that was located in the area.

The museum displays chart the development of currency from Ancient Japan through to modern day. Exhibits include currency related items, such as Edo-period wallets and coin purses disguised as sword hilts.

There are a variety of interactive exhibits. If you've ever wondered what a million yen weighs, this is your chance to find out! The souvenir shop has a variety of money-themed gifts.

Komparu-yu

 Tokyo Metro: Ginza Station

 460 yen

〒104-0061 東京都中央区銀座8-7-5
8-7-5 Ginza, Chuo-ku, Tokyo Postcode: 104-0061

14:00-22:00 (Closed Sundays & National Holidays)

Tucked away between a vending machine and a kimono store is an interesting survival: the public bathhouse Komparu-yu is a retro bath-house that hasn't changed much since it was built in 1863.

The building is as much of a treat as the baths, featuring some delightful murals, including swimming carp and several views of Mt. Fuji.

This bathhouse is so iconic, it featured in the manga series and later movie, *Thermae Romae.*

Upon entering the bathhouse, you put your shoes in a locker and head to the reception to pay. The bathhouse is segregated with separate sections for men and women. Remove your clothes in the changing room, taking only your towel and toiletries into the bathroom—no swimsuits.

Japanese baths are a place to relax rather than to wash.

There is a washing room with shower stations for you to wash your body before entering the bath. Only when you are clean should you enter the bath. There is a hot bath with a temperature of 42 degrees Celsius, and a warm bath.

You can rent a towel or purchase toiletries from the reception desk.

Tsukiji Hongan-ji

 Tokyo Metro: Tsukiji Station

 Free. Donations welcome.

 〒104-8435 東京都中央区築地3-15-1 (3-15-1 Tsukiji, Chuo-ku, Tokyo Postcode 104-8435)

 tsukijihongwanji.jp

6:00-16:00.

Tsukiji's Hongan-ji temple (also romanized as Hongwan-ji) is one of Tokyo's most striking temples architecturally.

The original temple was built in 1617 in Asakusa, in a distinctively Indian style. After the temple burnt down in 1657, it was relocated to an island of reclaimed land, Tsukiji, where it stood until being destroyed by the Great Kanto earthquake.

The current temple was rebuilt in 1934 and is the biggest Buddhist training center in the Kanto region.

Drawing on its past, the current temple was inspired by South Asian architecture. The stone exterior draws together elements of Buddhist, Hindu and Islamic architectural styles, while the wide columns show the influence of Greek temples.

The main building incorporates stained glass windows and a European-style pipe organ, while the interior maintains a distinctively Japanese feel.

The pipe organ is used in the monthly pipe organ concert, held 12:20-12:50, on the last Friday of the month. Admission is free.

Hama-rikyu Gardens

 Toei: Shiodome Station (7 mins) JR and Tokyo Metro: Shimbashi Station (13 mins)

 300 yen

 東京都中央区浜離宮庭園1-1 (1-1 Hamarikyuteien, Chuo, Tokyo Postcode: 104-0046)

 tokyo-park.or.jp

 09:00-17:00

Hama-rikyu Gardens is a traditional style Japanese garden on the edge of Tokyo harbor. The garden is surrounded by water on three sides.

Hama-rikyu makes the most of its unique location with several seawater ponds that raise and lower with the tides. The gardens are also a stop for the Tokyo Water Bus on its route from Asakusa.

Hama-rikyu was once the residence of a feudal lord, who used the grounds to hunt ducks. During another period, it was part of the imperial palace grounds with a detached palace built on the site. Traces of its history remain in the well-defined moat and two duck hunting blinds.

Many visitors consider the highlight of Hama-rikyu the tea-house, *Nakajima-no-ochaya* (tea house of the middle island), which serves matcha, powdered green tea, and sweets in the style of the tea ceremony.

Hama-rikyu has a selection of attractions throughout the year, especially in spring when the plum and cherry blossom is in bloom, later followed by fields of peony and flowering canola plants. In autumn, the park boasts beautiful maple and gingko leaves.

Eat

Ladurée Salon de Thé
Nearest Station: Tokyo Metro Ginza Station
Phone: 03-3563-2120
Address: 〒104-8212 東京都中央区銀座4-6-16 三越銀座店 (Mitsukoshi Ginza store, Ginza 4-6-16, Chuo-ku, Tokyo Postcode: 104-8212)
Hours: 10:30-22:00
Website: www.laduree.com

Paris comes to Tokyo with Ladurée. Nestled on the second floor of the Mitsukoshi department store, Ladurée offers delicious decadence in charming rococo surroundings.

Ladurée is a Parisian patisserie and tea house famous for inventing the macaron. The Ginza salon offers a selection of Ladurée's signature macarons, along with delicate pastries that have to be seen to be believed. Accompanying the sweets are a selection of Ladurée teas.

For a truly indulgent afternoon, bring a friend and split the afternoon tea set for two (¥7,260). This set includes fresh juice, macarons, tea and a selection of sweet and savory pastries and sandwiches.

Prices start at ¥800 for individual patisseries. Ladurée is popular, especially at weekends, so get there early to avoid a long wait.

Tsukishima Monjya Street
Nearest Station: Tokyo Metro and Toei: Tsukishima Station
Phone: 03-3532-1990
Address: 東京都中央区月島3-16-10 (3 Chome-16-10 Tsukishima, Chuo-ku, Tokyo Postcode: 104-0052)
Hours: Varies from restaurant to restaurant, but approximately 11:00-23:00
Website: www.monja.gr.jp

Tsukishima is an area of Tokyo that survived the Great Kanto earthquake. Although a lot of it has been developed, pockets of old-Tokyo survive. One of those is Monjya Street. Monjya is Tokyo's answer to the *Japanese* fast food staple *oknomiyaki*, a savory cross between pancake and pizza, and Tsukishima is the place to try it.

Monjya Street is lined with shops offering you the chance to cook your own *monjya*. Most of the restaurants have tables with grills built into them.

Monjya is mainly composed of a batter of flour and finely diced cabbage. You order your chosen toppings from the menu and are served them ready mixed. All you have to do is cook your *monjya* on the grill and enjoy.

Stay

Mandarin Oriental Tokyo
Nearest Station: Tokyo Metro: Mitsukoshimae Station
Phone: 03-3270-8800
Address: 〒103-8328 東京都中央区日本橋室町2-1-1 (2-1-1 Nihonbashi Muromachi, Chuo-ku Postcode:103-8328)
Website: mandarinoriental.com/tokyo/

Mandarin Oriental is a luxurious 5-star accommodation option, right in the heart of Tokyo. Located in Nihonbashi, the historic hub of Tokyo, the Mandarin Oriental hotel offers incredible views, every possible amenity, and an incredibly comfortable stay. Rooms start at ¥49,000 for a deluxe double room.

Sumisho Hotel
Nearest Station: Tokyo Metro: Ningyocho Station
Phone: 03-3661-4603
Address: 〒103-0024 東京都中央区日本橋小舟町9-14 (9-14 Kobuna-cho, Nihonbashi, Chuo-ku, Tokyo Postcode:103-0024)
Website: www.sumisho-hotel.co.jp

For a more affordable accommodation option that doesn't sacrifice location, Sumisho Hotel is a 3-star comfortable option for travelers wanting to be based in the Nihonbashi area.

This Japanese-style hotel offers guests the option of a communal Japanese style bath with optional *yukata* (light kimono), in addition to the Western-style bathroom attached to each room. A single room starts at ¥7,700. Japanese-style rooms are also available.

Central: Minato

Minato means 'port'—no prizes for guessing where this Tokyo ward is located! Minato includes not only Tokyo Bay and the islands within it, most notably the technological playground of Odaiba, but also Roppongi, a hilly area overlooking Tokyo, famous for its nightlife and foreign population.

See and Do
Tokyo Tower

 Toei Subway : Akabanebashi Station (5 mins)
Tokyo Metro: Kamiyacho Station (7 mins)

¥ Main observatory: 1,200 yen

 〒105-0011 東京都港区芝公園4-4-7 東京タワー
4 Chome-2-8 Shibakoen, Minato, Tokyo Postcode: 105-0011

🕐 9:00-23:00

🌐 tokyotower.co.jp

The Tokyo Skytree may have replaced Tokyo Tower as the city's tallest structure and the TV and radio broadcasting facility, but this iconic tourist destination is still worth a visit.

With reduced crowds since the opening of the Skytree, the 333m high Tokyo Tower offers amazing views over Tokyo, in particular, nearby Zojo-ji Temple, without the long waits of the Skytree.

Tokyo Tower was the tallest free-standing tower in the world when it was completed in 1958, being 13 meters taller than the Eiffel tower, on which it is based.

The tower's colorful orange and white exterior is in keeping with the aviation laws of its time.

Directly below Tokyo Tower is 'Foot Town,' a four-story building housing cafés,

restaurants, shopping and 'One Piece Tower,' an indoor amusement park themed around the popular Japanese comic series 'One Piece.'

Access to the 'Top Deck' as well as the main observatory is ¥2,800. Discounts are available for children and students.

Toyosu Fish Market Tuna Auctions

 Yurikamome Line: Shijō-mae Station

¥ Free

 〒135-0061 東京都江東区豊洲６丁目６
6 Chome-6 Toyosu, Koto City, Tokyo 135-0061, Japan

🕐 03:00-12:00. Closed Sundays.

 www.pia.co.jp/ssl/cgi-bin/ genform/form.cgi?ptn=toyosu

A visit to a fish market may seem like an unusual thing to do, but when you remember how integral fish is to the Japanese diet things make more sense.

For years, Tokyo's visitors had another market - Tsukiji - listed as one of the must-dos for the visit. Since 2018,

however, the famed tuna auctions have been held at this new location.

The experience is now more sanitized and less messy as you look down onto the tuna auction instead of being on the floor in the action. To see the action from this new viewing area,

enter the lottery using the website listed above one month in advance. If you win you will be one of 120 people allowed in for a 10-minute slot between 5:45am and 6:15am. There is also a second viewing gallery further from the action which does not require reservations.

Boat Cruise

 Yurikamome Line: Hinode Station
JR: Hamamatsucho Station (8 mins)

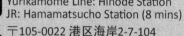 〒105-0022 港区海岸2-7-104
Minato-ku, Kaigan 2-7-104 Postcode: 015-0022

 Gozabune Atakemaru: Cruises at 12:40/17:05/19:35

 Gozabune Atakemaru:From ¥2,600 at lunch per adult.

 gozabune.jp

There are many boat cruises on offer in Tokyo, allowing you to enjoy a different view of Tokyo Bay and its many rivers.

One of the best ways to take in the harbor is by combining your river cruise with a trip to the reclaimed island, Odaiba, with its myriad of attractions and the striking Rainbow Bridge.

Perhaps the most unique of the many cruises on offer is Gozabune Atakemaru, and Edo-period style boat that offers a simple cruise during the day and two evening cruises featuring a comedy show in Kabuki-style, one of which includes an all you can eat and drink dinner buffet for ¥9,200.

Other cruise options include the Tokyo water bus's simple river transit options, or houseboats that offer dinner on board, especially popular in the summer during firework festivals.

Odaiba

 Yurikamome Line: Daiba, Tokyo Teleport or Kokusai Tenjiro

 〒135-0064 東京都 江東区青海2-3-6 (2-3-6 Aomi, Koto-ku, Tokyo Postcode:135-0064)

bit.ly/odaibaarea

Most buildings are open 10:00 to 21:00

Odaiba began life as an artificial island, constructed in 1853 as a platform for cannons, a defense against foreign invasion. Odaiba now welcomes visitors as a glitzy showcase of all Tokyo has to offer.

Odaiba has three parts. Firstly, it is a shopper's paradise with multiple mega malls, including Venice-themed Venus Fort, Divers City, Aqua City and Tokyo Decks.

Next, it is a signpost of Japanese innovation, whether in the stunning modern architecture of the headquarters of Fuji TV and Telekom Center, or in the displays and exhibits of Miraikan, the National Museum of Emerging Science and Innovation.

Finally, Odaiba is a leisure destination, with a seaside park that meanders around the island, numerous arcades, movie theaters and other attractions.

There are two interactive digital art museums too - teamLab Planets and teamLab Borderless which are a must-visit for the Instagram generation (book well in advance).

It's also a hub of geek culture, with an 18-meter-tall statue of a Gundam, a battle robot from the anime of the same name, and Tokyo Big Sight, an exhibition center that hosts several massive anime and manga conventions.

Odaiba will play a major part in the 2021 Tokyo Olympics as the host of the triathlon and marathon swimming competitions.

Odaiba Kaihin Koen (Seaside Park)

 Yurikamome Line:Odaiba Kaihin Koen Station

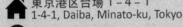 ¥ Free

🏠 東京港区台場１－４－１
1-4-1, Daiba, Minato-ku, Tokyo

🕐 24/7

🌐 tptc.co.jp

'Kaihin Koen' translates as 'seaside park,' and that is literally what Odaiba's Kaihin Koen is.

The beach is artificial and you cannot swim, but you can enjoy windsurfing, paddling, or simply walking along the sand.

The park feels spacious compared to other Tokyo parks and is rarely crowded.

Walking through the park you will see cannons dating from the Edo-period, Shiokaze park with its beautiful fountain, and - often confusingly for foreign visitors - a replica of the Statue of Liberty.

At night, the rainbow bridge is lit up.

Kaihin Koen is a stop on the water bus route, as well as the departure or arrival point for many Tokyo Bay cruises.

Zojoji Temple

 Tokyo Metro Hibiya Line: Shibakoen Station or Onarimon Station
Toei Subway: Daimon Station

 ¥ Free. Donations welcome.

 🏠 〒105-0011 東京都港区芝公園4-7-35
(Tokyo, Minato-ku, Shibakoen, 4-7-35, Postcode: 105-0011)

 🌐 zojoji.or.jp

 🕐 9:00-17:00

Zojo-ji temple flourished during the Edo-period as the family temple and later mausoleum of the Tokugawa shoguns. Six of the fifteen Tokugawa shoguns are buried in mausoleums in the temple grounds.

In contrast to the formal graves, there is a section of the graveyard dedicated to children who died before or shortly after birth. The cemetery consists of rows of Jizo statues, dressed in bright caps and bibs by parents, often with offerings of presents and toys nearby.

Today, Zojo-ji is the main temple of the *Jodo shu* school of Buddhism. Like most of Tokyo's temples, Zojo-ji is a reconstruction of an earlier temple destroyed by disasters. However, the main entrance gate Sangedatsumon has survived intact from 1622.

The gate's name refers to the belief that passing through it will free you from three earthly evils—greed, anger and stupidity. Try it and see if it works.

Oedo Onsen Monogatari

 Free shuttle bus from Tokyo-Teleport Stn, Tokyo Station & Shinagawa Station

 Mon-Fri ¥2,720, Weekends ¥2,936, Peak Period ¥3,044.

 〒135-0064東京都江東区青海2丁目6番3号 (2-6-3 Aomi, Koto-ku Tokyo Postcode: 135-0064)

 daiba.ooedoonsen.jp

24/7 except 09:00-11:00

Oedo Onsen Monogatari describes itself as an *onsen* (Japanese hot spring) theme park. The attraction combines bath and beauty spa with Edo-inspired restaurants and entertainment in Odaiba. It's not a bath, more a bathing experience.

When you arrive, you choose a *yukata* (light *kimono*) to wear inside the *onsen* building. Leaving your modern clothes and luggage behind in your locker, you can relax and enjoy the atmosphere of an Edo-period festival.

Just like a Japanese festival, there are several snack and game stalls set up, featuring traditional entertainments, such as fishing with paper nets for prizes or throwing ninja-style stars for prizes.

The restaurants are similarly old-Japan themed. You can choose from Japanese-style street foods such as ramen and udon, chicken skewers and sushi, to a *kaiseki* (traditional high cuisine) meal in a private room.

The main attraction is the baths. These are Japanese style, segregated between

male and female, and intended for relaxation. You wash before you enter the bath, and there are no towels or swimsuits permitted in the bath itself. If this is your first *onsen*, relax! There are English instructions, so you can bathe with confidence. Like many baths, Oedo Onsen Monogatari prohibits customers with tattoos.

After your bath, you can relax by dozing in one of the many lounges, go for a stroll in the garden, take in a foot bath or treat yourself to one of the many spa treatments.

Nezu Museum

 Tokyo Metro: Omotesando Station (8 mins)

 Special Exhibit: 1300 yen, General Exhibit: 1100 yen

 6 Chome-5-1 Minamiaoyama, Minato City, Tokyo 107-0062, Japan

10:00-17:00 (Closed Mondays)

 nezu-muse.or.jp

Nezu Museum is a stunning collection of over 7400 Chinese bronzes, Korean ceramics and Japanese calligraphy. The museum houses its collection in an incredible modern building that melds traditional

design elements to modern materials and techniques and is an artwork in its own right.

The museum was founded by Nezu Kaichiro, president of the Tobu Railway

company and is located on the site of the Nezu family's residence.

The museum's collection includes seven national treasures and 87 important cultural properties.

Mori Art Museum

 Tokyo Metro & Toei: Roppongi Station

 2,000 yen (entrance to the Observation Deck)

 東京港区六本木６−１０−１六本木ヒルズ森タワー
Roppongi Hills Mori Tower 6-10-1 Roppongi, Minato-ku, Tokyo

 Wednesday-Monday: 10:00-22:00, Tuesday: 10:00-17:00 (last entry 30 minutes before closing)

mori.art.museum

The Mori Art Museum is located on the fifty-third floor of the Mori Tower in Roppongi Hills.

The art museum focuses on contemporary art and is unusual in that it doesn't have a permanent collection. When there are no exhibits, the museum closes.

The Mori Art Museum features a large number of international artists, and accordingly attracts a large number of foreign tourists - perfect if you want a palette cleanser between looking at woodcuts and temples.

Along with the nearby National Art Center and Suntory Museum of Art, Mori Art Museum makes up the Roppongi Art Triangle.

Tokyo City View Observation Deck

 Tokyo Metro and Toei: Roppongi Station

 Sky deck - 500 yen

 東京港区六本木６−１０−１六本木ヒルズ森タワー
(Roppongi Hills Mori Tower 6-10-1 Roppongi, Minato-ku, Tokyo)

roppongihills.com

 Sky Deck: 13:00-22:00

Mori Tower is a skyscraper dominating the Roppongi Hills.

Completed in 2003, the 54-floor building features multiple attractions, including the Tokyo City View Observation Deck which is on the 52nd floor, and offers views of Tokyo from 218 meters.

Advance tickets to the Observation deck are available and enable the holder to move directly through the ticket gate, bypassing any queues.

The Sky Deck on the 54th-floor is open-air, offering unrestricted 360-degree views of Tokyo from 238 meters.

Before entering the Sky Deck, the staff will check that you are not carrying anything that might be blown away. There are lockers available to store your possessions.

The deck is not wheelchair friendly or recommended for small children. During bad weather, the Sky Deck may be closed.

Madame Tussauds Tokyo

 Yurikamome Line: Odaiba Kaihin Koen Station

 1,800 yen (online - 2,300 on the door)

 〒135-0091東京都港区台場1-6-1デックス東京ビーチアイランドモール3F (Odaiba 1-6-1 Decks Tokyo Beach Island Mall 3F, Minato-ku, Tokyo, Postcode: 135-0091)

 madametussauds.jp

 10:00-20:00 (last entry 19:00)

London's iconic waxworks expanded to Tokyo in 2013, with Madame Tussauds Tokyo.

The selection of celebrities on offer includes a mixture of Japanese and International celebrities.

You can take your photo with lifelike wax models of celebrities, including pop stars like Lady Gaga or members of Japan's AKB48, sporting legends like Yu Darvish, world leaders like the Dalai Lama, and celebrity icons like Elvis and Marilyn Monroe.

Sengaku-ji

 Toei Subway: Sengakuji Station

 Free but a donation to the temple is welcome

 〒108-0074 東京都港区高輪2-11-1 2-11-1 Takanawa, Minato-ku, Tokyo Postcode: 108-0074

 April-September: 7:00-18:00, October-March: 7:00-17:00

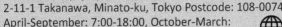 sengakuji.or.jp

Sengaku-ji was known as one of the three major temples of Edo, but today is better known as the resting place of the 47 ronin. A ronin is a master-less samurai.

The 47 ronin served Asano Naganori, a feudal lord of the seventeenth-century. During an altercation with a rival within Edo-castle, Asano drew his sword. It was a crime to draw a weapon in the Imperial Palace, and Asano was ordered to commit ritual suicide. He was buried at Sengaku-ji.

Upon his death, Asano's samurai were declared ronin. They decided to avenge their former master by killing his rival and bringing his head to Sengaku-ji. As punishment for this crime, the shogun ordered the 47 ronin to commit suicide. All 47 ronin are buried with their lord within the temple grounds.

The temple houses many artifacts related to the 47 ronin, including their clothing and armor.

Japanese language videos bring the legend to life.

The graveyard is located at the south of the temple grounds and is small and somber. Asano's grave is nearby in a fenced-off enclosure.

Also of interest is the *suikinkutsu*, a Japanese style garden ornament that combines a water feature with a musical instrument. Ladling water through a hole in an inverted pot produces a sound rather like that of *koto*, a Japanese lute.

Akasaka Palace

 Tokyo Metro and JR: Yotsuya Station (7 mins)

 Garden: 300 yen, Main Building: 1,500 yen, Japanese-Style Annex: 1,500 yen

 〒100-8914東京都千代田区永田町1-6-1 (1-6-1 Nagata-cho, Chiyoda-ku, Tokyo Postcode: 100-8914)

 www8.cao.go.jp

 See description

Akasaka Palace was originally built as an imperial residence for the Crown Prince in 1909. The Imperial family ceded the palace following WWII.

The palace is now administered by the Japanese government who use it as housing for visiting foreign dignitaries.

It has only recently opened to the public, but entry to the main building is limited to 1500 people a day. To get inside or to tour the Japanese-Style Annex apply in advance online through the palace's official website. The palace grounds are always open.

The palace is one of the biggest buildings constructed during the Meiji period and is closely modeled on Buckingham Palace. It is Japan's only neo-baroque style palace.

Unfortunately, no photos of the palace's exquisite interior are allowed. You have to see it for yourself.

Operating Hours:
* Garden: 10:00-17:00 (last entry 16:30)
* Main Building: 10:00 to 17:00
* Japanese Style Annex: Six 40-minute tours conducted at hourly intervals from 10:30-15:00 (The English tour is at 15:00)

Teien Art Museum

 Toei Subway: Shirokanedai Station (6 mins)
JR: Meguro Station (7 mins)

 Garden: 100 yen
Main Building: Depends on exhibitions

 〒108-0071 東京都港区白金台5-21-9
5-21-9, Shirokanedai, Minato-ku, Tokyo Postcode: 108-0071

 10:00-18:00 (closed second and fourth Wednesdays and New Years)

 teien-art-museum.ne.jp

If you can't get inside the Akasaka palace, consider another former Imperial residence.

The Tokyo Teien Art Museum is a glorious art-deco masterpiece that started life as the residence of Prince Asaka Yasuhiko.

After WWII, it became first the residence of the prime minister, then the official state guest house until the small size of the building led to its current incarnation as an art museum.

Although few of the palace's furnishings remain, the elegant chandeliers and building design evoke the building in its heyday. The exhibitions vary, but visiting is worth it for the house alone.

Eat

Tokyo Shiba Tofuya-ukai
Nearest Station: Toei Subway: Akabanebashi Station (5 mins), Tokyo Metro: Shiba-Koen Station (7 mins)
Phone: 03-3436-1028
Address: 〒105-0011東京都港区芝公園4-4-13 (4-4-13 Shiba-koen, Minato-ku, Tokyo Postcode: 105-0011)
Hours: 11:00-20:00, closed one Monday every month
Website: www.ukai.co.jp

A stone's throw from Tokyo tower is Tofuya-ukai, a gourmet restaurant that prides itself on its tofu dishes. Tofu is hand-made and served as part of an exquisite *kaiseki* menu.

Kaiseki is a multi-course meal featuring many small dishes with seasonal ingredients prepared along traditional Japanese lines. This is not fast food. Linger over your meal, savoring the ingredients and atmosphere.

The restaurant has *tatami* (sat on the floor) sections as well as tables. All courses include Tofuya-ukai's signature dishes. Hand-made tofu served in a soymilk broth, and slices of deep-fried tofu served with sweet miso. Lunch starts at ¥6,450 (¥8,100 at weekends), dinner courses start at ¥6,450. Courses can be made vegetarian on request - call ahead.

L'Atelier de Joël Robuchon
Nearest Station: Tokyo Metro and Toei Subway: Roppongi Station
Phone: 03-5772-7500
Address: 〒106-0032 東京都港区六本木6-10-1 六本木ヒルズ ヒルサイド 2 F (2F Hillside, Roppongi Hills, 6-10-1 Roppongi, Minato-ku, Tokyo 106-0032)
Hours: Lunch: Weekdays 11:30-14:30, Weekends and National Holidays 11:30-15:00. Dinner: 18:00-21:30.
Website: www.robuchon.jp

Sample world-class French cuisine at an affordable price. Joël Robuchon is a renowned chef with a string of restaurants in Tokyo, all of which offer a different dining experience.

Reservations are necessary. Lunch starts at ¥3,500, and dinner at ¥5,300, with the special seasonal degustation course costing ¥18,900.

For something cheaper, there is a bakery with bread, pastries and cakes.

Stay

The Ritz-Carlton Tokyo
Nearest Station: Tokyo Metro: Roppongi Station
Phone: 03-3423-8000
Address: 〒107-0052東京都港区赤坂９－７－１東京ミッドタウン (Tokyo Midtown 9-7-1 Akasaka Minato-ku Tokyo Postcode: 107-6245)
Website: ritzcarlton.com

The Ritz-Carlton Tokyo delivers guests an outstanding experience. The five-star hotel boasts a day spa with an indoor swimming pool, jacuzzi overlooking Tokyo tower, and a variety of spa treatments.

The restaurants showcase the best of Japanese food alongside stunning views of Mt Fuji, or offer fine French dining or light cafe fare. The bar hosts occasional jazz performances.

The Ritz-Carlton's rooms come at five-star prices. Prices start at ¥41,400 for the deluxe guest room.

Kasuga Ryokan
Nearest Station: Toei Subway: Akabanebashi Station (5 mins), Tokyo Metro: Shibakoen Station (7 mins), Monorail: Hamamatsu-cho Station (5 mins)
Phone: 03-3451-1443
Address: 〒105-0011 東京都港区芝3-4-18 (3-43-18 Shiba Minato-ku Tokyo Postcode:105-0014)
Website: biglobe.ne.jp/kasuga/

Kasuga Ryokan is a 2-STAR traditional Japanese style hotel located near Tokyo Tower.

Kasuga Ryokan retains the look and feel of the Showa-era. Upon entering the ryokan, visitors remove their shoes and step into *geta*, traditional wooden sandals.

The rooms are Japanese style. Guests sleep on futons on the tatami floor. Note there are only squat toilets.

The ryokan has gender-segregated communal baths. The rates start at ¥5,500 for one person, no meals. Cash only.

Shinjuku

Shinjuku has numerous claims to fame. Since 1991 when the Tokyo Government moved to Shinjuku, the ward has been Tokyo's political center. It is home to the Tokyo Government Buildings and the busiest train station in the world. While these might not sound like exciting draws, Shinjuku has exciting nightlife and some surprising tourist attractions, starting with the ward's tourism ambassador - Godzilla himself.

See and Do

Kabuki-cho (Godzilla Head, King Kong)

 JR, Tokyo Metro and Toei: Shinjuku Station

 Free to walk around. Most bars have a cover charge.

 東京都新宿区歌舞伎町 (Kabukicho, Shinjuku-ku, Tokyo)

 kabukicho.or.jp

 Most restaurants and bars open 17:00-23:00.

Kabuki-cho is a colorful night-life district, with over 3000 bars (including host and hostess bars), cabarets, nightclubs, love hotels, and karaoke parlors.

It is located around Yasukuni-dori (Yasukuni avenue). Its seedy reputation leads to it being known as Tokyo's red-light district. Despite this, and the fact that Kabuki-cho is believed to be a center of *yakuza* (the Japanese mafia) influence, the area is astonishingly safe for tourists. Stay alert and if you feel uncomfortable, settle your bill and leave.

During the day, the gaudy signs of Kabuki-cho draw visitors. Two, in particular, stand out. Hotel Gracery's Godzilla peeks over the hotel walls, no doubt biding his time to attack. King Kong swings from a building down one of Kabuki-cho's many side streets.

At night, Kabuki-cho really comes alive with neon signs and bustling crowds. It's a good idea to come with plenty of cash as many of Kabuki-cho's hole in the wall style bars don't accept credit or debit cards.

Hosts and Hostesses, dressed in their finery, call out to pedestrians, trying to entice them into their clubs.

Get an idea of the price before you commit yourself. Host and Hostess bars can be very pricey, and some of the other bars have a hefty cover charge.

To help foreign tourists navigate Kabuki-cho, hotel concierges in Shinjuku have put together a register of businesses that will provide a fun night out without any shady dealing. Ask your hotel for recommendations.

Alternatively, consider a guided tour. These can be booked from the Tokyo Tourist Information Center, Shinjuku (3F BUSTA Shinjuku).

Shinjuku Gyoen National Garden

 Toei Subway:
Tochomae Station
JR and Tokyo Metro:
Shinjuku Station

 Free

 〒160-0014 東京都
新宿区内藤町１ 1
(11 Naitomachi,
Shinjuku, Tokyo
Postcode: 160-0014)

 bit.ly/Shinjukugyoen

 09:30-16:30 (winter),
09:30-19:00 (summer)

Shinjuku Gyoen is beautiful no matter what time of year you visit.

In spring, busy Tokyo office workers flock to enjoy the ephemeral cherry blossoms while they last.

In summer, you can beat the heat with a lazy picnic beneath the shade of the many trees.

In autumn, the changing leaves provide a striking contrast to the bland steel and glass of the skyscrapers beyond.

If you arrive too late for the November chrysanthemums, don't be tempted to skip the park. The garden is so carefully landscaped that it is worth visiting even in winter.

In addition, the greenhouses with their collection of tropical plants, and the two cafés and traditional tea house, never go out of season.

Shinjuku Gyoen is a great place to recharge your energy or to recover from the stress of navigating busy Shinjuku station.

Samurai Museum

 Tokyo Metro and Toei: Higashi-Shinjuku Station (6 mins)
JR: Shinjuku Station (10 mins)

 東京都新宿区歌舞伎町2-25-6
Shinjuku-ku, Tokyo Kabukicho 2-25-6

 10:30-21:00 (last entry 20:30)

 1900 yen

 samuraimuseum.jp

The Samurai Museum is a foreigner-friendly museum designed to introduce visitors to 800 years of samurai history.

The museum is small, but uses that to its advantage, offering targeted exhibits in settings that subtly recreate the ambiance of the samurai period.

The museum's owner spent five years collating the museum's collection. His goal is to educate visitors about the reality of the samurai lifestyle, and revive the soul of the samurai.

To that end, the Samurai Museum has some attractions you won't find at a bigger, more serious

museum. You can dress in samurai armor and have your photo taken. You can also see a demonstration of sword drawing, or try your hand at calligraphy.

This friendly museum is a must, for students of Japanese history and the casual visitor alike.

Ninja Trick House

 Tokyo Metro and Toei: Higashi-Shinjuku Station (8 mins)
JR: Shinjuku Station (13 mins)

¥ 1650 yen

 東京都新宿区歌舞伎町 2-28-13 第一和幸ビル 4F
First Kazuyuki building 4, Kabukicho 2-28-13, Shinjuku-ku, Tokyo

🕐 10:00-18:00 (last entry 17:00). Closed Wednesdays and some Tuesdays.

🌐 ninja-trick-house.com

The Ninja Trick House is only a few blocks away from the Samurai museum, but it is a very different experience.

The Ninja Trick House is activity-based. Groups are limited to four, and taken through by a guide who demonstrates the activities and explains their context within the ninja's life.

The activities - a ninja scavenger hunt, sword practice and *shuriken* (pointed metal disc) throwing - take an adult on their own roughly half an hour to complete, but a family with children may find it takes 45 minutes to move through the house.

There are plenty of opportunities for photos.

If this taste of Ninja life is not enough, or you wanting some specialized practice, consider heading to the nearby Ninja Club Shinjuku Gym. Sessions are ¥3,000 per person for the ninja experience, or ¥5,000 for 60 minutes of personal training. You must reserve in advance, either by phone (070-4217-3915, 15:00-24:00) or e-mail (shinjuku.gym@gmail.com).

Tokyo Metropolitan Government Buildings

 JR: Sendagaya Station (5 mins) or Shinjuku Station (10 mins)
Tokyo Metro: Shinjuku Gyoenmae Station (5 mins)

¥ Free

🏠 〒163-8001 東京都新宿区西新宿２丁目８−1
2 Chome-8-1 Nishishinjuku, Shinjuku City, Tokyo 163-8001, Japan

🕐 09:00-23:00

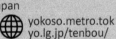 yokoso.metro.tokyo.lg.jp/tenbou/

If The Tokyo SkyTree or Tokyo Tower are out of your price range, head to Shinjuku.

The Tokyo Metropolitan Government Building Observation Deck offers the best free view of Tokyo from its political center. Simply take the Observatory Elevator from the first floor of the main building.

On fine days, the 202m high platforms allow you to see as far away as Mount Fuji. Nearer highlights include the Tokyo Dome, Skytree, Tokyo Tower and Meiji Jingu Shrine.

There are two observatories, located in the North and South towers. Both have cafés and restaurants (careful—these

are not budget-friendly!), and the North tower observatory stays open later, with views of Tokyo at night.

As it is a government building, security measures are in place. Be prepared for a bag search and carry your passport in case it is required.

Meiji Jingu Baseball Stadium

 Tokyo Metro: Gaienmae Station
Toei: Kokuritsu-Kyogijo Station

 See description

 東京都新宿区霞ケ丘町3-1 (3-1, Kasumigaokacho, Shinjuku, Tokyo)

 jingu-stadium.com

 Game days: 11:00 to 20 mins after the game, Non-Game days: 11:00-17:00

Sumo may be Japan's national sport, but baseball is its most popular. Fans of the game have been visiting Meiji Jingu stadium since 1926. The historic stadium is home to the Yakult Swallows, a professional baseball team competing in Japan's major league, as well as numerous college and high school games.

Jingu Baseball Stadium is one of the few surviving stadiums that Babe Ruth played at.

Even if you're not a baseball fan, catching a Japanese baseball game is an experience. The large crowds are incredibly well-behaved, and they encourage their team with displays of coordinated cheering. Yakult Swallows supporters, for instance, bring umbrellas to cheer their team.

After the fans, the cheerleaders, a tradition imported from America, feel like an anti-climax.

You can take your chances and buy your ticket at the gate on the day, but if you want to be sure of getting a seat, tickets can be bought in advance through convenience stores.

The stadium has a variety of food options, including an American BBQ stand.

Prices start at ¥1,800 for a basic seat in the outfield, and go up to ¥5,900 for one in a prime location.

Shin-Okubo Korea Town

 JR Yamanote Line: Shin-Okubo Station   Free

 Tonchang restaurant, for example: 東京都新宿区百人町2-1-4盛好堂ビル2F
2F Shigeyoshitou-biru Hyakunin-cho 2-1-4, Shinjuku-ku, Tokyo

The area surrounding Shin-Okubo is home to a vibrant community of Koreans, packing around 350 restaurants into a tiny area of Tokyo.

Shin-Okubo offers spicy food and a lively nightlife. Highlights include Korean style BBQ houses, markets offering authentic Korean alcohol and cooking ingredients, and fun and tasty street food.

You won't have trouble finding a good meal, but if you want a tried and true favorite, Korean BBQ house Tomchang Shinokubo Bekkan is a crowd-pleaser. Details are above.

For fans of Korean pop-culture, in particular K-pop (Korean pop music), Shin-Okubo is a must-visit. There are karaoke bars that specialize in K-pop music and numerous stores selling

merchandise of your favorite Korean bands. You may even see a genuine K-Pop group handing out fliers for their performances.

In recent years, Shin-Okubo has made room for some new businesses. You can now find a selection of halal groceries and restaurants in what is becoming known as *Yokocho*, or 'Islam alley.'

Eat

Tokyo Robot Restaurant
Nearest Station: JR Lines/ Tokyo Metro/Toei Subway: Shinjuku Station
Phone: 03-3200-5500
Address: 東京都新宿区歌舞伎町1-7-1 新宿ロボットビルB2F (B2F Shinjuku Robot Bldg, 1-7-1 Kabukicho Shinjuku-ku, Tokyo)
Hours: 16:00-22:00 (Shows at set times).
Website: shinjuku-robot.com

Tokyo Robot Restaurant is a modern variation on the cabaret performances that were once a big part of Kabuki-cho's nightlife. The entire building pulses with light, energy and music.

The food is not great—your choice of three *bento* (packed lunches) and a bottle of water, but you're there for the show, a 90-minute performance by robots and dancing girls.

The entrance fee is ¥8,500, the meal fee ¥1,000-1,500. Reserve in advance (discounts are available).

Omoide Yokocho
Nearest Station: JR Lines/ Tokyo Metro/Toei Subway: Shinjuku Station
Address: 東京都新宿区西新宿１－２－６ (1-2-6 Nishi-Shinjuku, Shinjuku-ward, Tokyo)
Hours: Generally 17:00-0:00.
Website: shinjuku-omoide.com

Omoide Yokocho, 'nostalgia alley,' is a small section of Shinjuku where the tiny streets with even tinier eateries resist attempts to modernize and develop the district. The main attraction is the *yakitori* restaurants/ bars, selling meat (mostly chicken) grilled on skewers right before you, and drinks.

These small bars offer an intimate dining experience, as their size (many can only seat 6-8 customers), makes for a convivial atmosphere. Some bars reserve their seats for regular patrons, so don't be offended if you are turned away. Instead, try the next! Some bars have a cover charge. *Taro* has English menus.

If you find the atmosphere claustrophobic but want to try some *yakitori*, head back into Kabuki-cho for *Don-Don Yakiniku*, a restaurant with English menus and photos of the food on offer. You cook your own meat on a *hibachi*, a pot filled with coals (Don-Don Yakiniku 03-5155 3580 / 新宿区歌舞伎町１－２３－１３塩村ビル１Ｆ・Shimomura Bldg 1F 1-23-13 Kabuki-dori Kabukicho Shinjuku).

Stay

Hotel Gracery Shinjuku
Nearest Station: JR, Tokyo Metro and Toei Subway: Shinjuku Station
Phone: 03-6833-2489
Address: 東京都新宿区歌舞伎町1-19-1 (1-19-1 Kabukicho, Shinjuku-ku, Tokyo)
Website: shinjuku.gracery.com

Hotel Gracery is perhaps the only hotel in the world to offer the dubious pleasure of getting up close to a legendary monster, with rooms allowing you to look out at Godzilla—and Godzilla to look in.

For true monster aficionados, the Godzilla penthouse on the top floor, has Godzilla's claw breaking

through the wall as well as a shrine of movie memorabilia.

A standard single starts at ¥15,700 a night (¥17,700 with breakfast), with a Godzilla view room ¥16,700 (¥18,700 with breakfast).

Shinjuku Kuyakusho-mae Capsule Hotel
Nearest Station: JR, Tokyo Metro and Toei Subway: Shinjuku Station
Phone: 03-3232-1110
Address: 東京都新宿区歌舞伎町１－２－５投与ビル３Ｆ (Touyo Bldg.3F, 1-2-5 Kabukicho, Shinjuku-ku, Tokyo)
Website: capsuleinn.com

Capsule Hotels are no-frills hotels that traditionally

targeted salarymen who missed the last train and needed a place to sleep and refresh themselves overnight.

The capsules have just enough room to lie down and sit up. You leave your luggage in lockers before heading to the lounge to relax, or to the male-only sauna and bathhouse. There is a female-only floor with a shower room. The 1-star capsules start at ¥3,500 a night.

Author's Note: "Although more comfortable than expected, I didn't find the capsule very restful, but it was definitely a cheaper option than a hotel."

Shibuya

Shibuya is a shopper's paradise, particularly for fashion fans. Not only is the district synonymous with the shopping district surrounding Shibuya Station, but it includes Harajuku, the center of youth culture, Omotesando, a stylish shopping street, and Sendagaya, the apparel district. Even if you are on a budget, Shibuya is still a fun place to visit. Window shopping costs nothing, and neither does people watching.

See and Do

Shibuya Pedestrian Crossing

 JR and Tokyo Metro: Shibuya Station

 Free

 〒150-0043 東京都渋谷区道玄坂1丁目12-1 渋谷マークシティ (Shibuya Mark City, Dogenzaka1-12-1, Shibuya-ku, Tokyo Postcode:150-0043)

Busiest between 10:00-21:00

Shibuya pedestrian crossing is synonymous with Tokyo itself. It features in movies, music videos and documentaries. No wonder, Shibuya is the busiest pedestrian crossing in the world.

The three giant advertising screens overlooking the crossing have become icons and led to comparisons to New York's Times Square, but the crossing itself is the attraction. Watching the busy intersection come to a complete halt for the crowds spilling out or into Shibuya station is a sight that never gets old.

To get to the crossing, head for the station's Hachiko exit.

Author's Note: "Head to the bridge linking Shinjuku station to Shibuya Mark City for a free view of the crossing in action (details above)."

Cat Street

 JR: Harajuku Station
Tokyo Metro: Meiji Jingu Mae 'Harajuku' Station

 〒150-0001 東京都渋谷区神宮前５丁目１０−１０
Jingu-mae 5-10-10, Shibuya-ku, Tokyo Postcode: 150-0001

 Free

 Varies from store to store, but generally 11:00-21:00

Cat Street is a pleasant, pedestrian boulevard that extends from Omotesando, all the way to Shibuya's Miyashita Park. It is lined with a selection of fashionable stores.

Shops range from upmarket fashion to funky teenage trends. American Apparel has two stores here, among Japanese boutiques offering a truly unique take on global trends.

It's not all clothes though. Candy Show Time is a handmade candy store, specializing in popping candies. You can watch the staff at work making the candy through a glass window.

Meiji Jingu and Yoyogi Park

 JR: Harajuku Station
Tokyo Metro: Meiji Jingu Mae 'Harajuku' Station

 Free, but donations are welcome.

 〒151−8557 東京都渋谷区代々木神園町１−１ (1-1 Yoyogikamizonocho Shibuya, Tokyo Postcode: 151-8557)

 meijijingu.or.jp

 Sunrise to sunset

Meiji Jingu Shrine is among the most important Shinto shrines in Japan, closely associated with the Imperial family.

The shrine is an oasis of calm and greenery in the center of one of Tokyo's busiest districts. As you relax in Yoyogi Park, surrounding the shrine, you have a hard time believing you are walking distance from the busiest pedestrian crossing in the world.

Meiji Jingu is an incredibly popular place to ring in the New Year. Hatsumode, the first shrine visit of the New Year, has special significance, and Meiji Jingu draws huge crowds in the early days of January.

Crowds begin to assemble on New Year's Eve, queuing in the cold for hours until midnight. Food stalls are set up along the long stone path approaching Meiji Jingu, and a festival air prevails. The rest of the year, Meiji Jingu is relatively low-key, a pleasant escape from the bustle of the surrounding shopping districts.

Meiji Jingu is especially nice to visit on the weekend. In addition to the chance of spotting a traditional Japanese wedding at the shrine, Yoyogi Park is the meeting point for the various subculture groups that center around Harajuku.

Yoyogi Park is worth a visit in its own right. It is divided into two areas. The forest park is great for activities, with space for skating, jogging and cycling (you can rent a bike within the park). There are wide open fields as well as the forested areas, a bird sanctuary, an observation deck that looks over the park.

The second part has a stadium and is a popular event venue. There's usually something happening, whether it's a concert, a sporting event, or even a flea market.

Shibuya Sky, Shibuya Scramble Square

 JR and Tokyo Metro: Shibuya Station

 1,800 online (2,000 on the day)

 〒150-0002 東京都渋谷区渋谷２丁目２４−12 最上階 スクランブルスクエア
〒150-0002 Tokyo, Shibuya City, Shibuya, 2 Chome−24−12

 10:00-23:00

 www.shibuya-scramble-square.com/sky/

Located high above the Shibuya crossing, Shibuya Sky is the newest observation center in Tokyo. It is pretty standard as these go and can be compared with Tokyo Tower and the Skytree - although here there is a fantastic open-air rooftop.

Elsewhere, the Shibuya Scramble Square building features restaurants with city views and stores.

Harajuku

 JR: Harajuku Station
Tokyo Metro: Meiji Jingu Mae 'Harajuku' Station

 東京都渋谷区神宮前１－１９－８ 竹下通り
Takeshita-dori, Jingu-mae 1-19-8, Shibuya-ku, Tokyo

¥ Free

Varies from store to store, but generally 11:00-21:00

Harajuku has been a center for youth subcultures since the 1970s. Although most often associated with the gothic lolita style, characterized by old-fashioned style, full skirts, elaborate hairstyles and an abundance of lace, you can find all manner of fashions on offer at Harajuku.

Traditionally, small, independent and quirky fashion boutiques lined Takeshita-dori, the main pedestrian street. Today, as big international chains like H&M and Forever 21 have made an appearance, many of the more quirky stores have moved to the side streets.

One big chain store worth checking out is the big Daiso on Takeshita-dori. Daiso is a chain of ¥100 stores, selling extremely cheap goods. The selection varies, but it is a good place to stock up on travel essentials like earplugs, eye masks and cooling scarves, as well as souvenirs for friends and family back home.

Harajuku has a fun atmosphere, though it can get crowded at the weekends. Not only fashion but international culture, in particular American pop culture, is celebrated here, and it is a fun place to shop - you never know what you'll find.

There is an ever-changing mix of restaurants, including some decent burger joints, some Mexican, and some decidedly untraditional sushi. Our recommendation is to treat yourself to a Harajuku tradition, a sweet crepe from a food stall.

Harajuku Station is also worth a look. Built in 1906, the station building is one of the few truly old stations to remain.

Meguro Parasitological Museum

 JR, Tokyo Metro and Toei Subway: Meguro Station (15 mins)

¥ Free

 153-0064　東京都目黒区下目黒4-1-1
4-1-1, Shimomeguro, Meguro-ku, Tokyo 153-0064

 10:00-17:00. Closed Mon, Tues. If Mon or Tues is a public holiday, the museum opens and closes the following day.

 www.kiseichu.org

The Meguro Parasitological Museum claims to be the only museum in the world dedicated to parasites - and that is probably right.

Founded in 1953 by Satoru Kamegai, a doctor with an interest in parasites, the two-story collection is delightfully old school. Many of the museum's 60,000 parasite specimens are stored in glass jars that were labeled by hand.

The first floor has displays and movies devoted to the diversity of parasites, but non-Japanese speakers will find the collection of Human and Zoonotic Parasites on the second floor much easier to understand - not that this is necessarily a good thing!

The world's longest tapeworm is particularly disturbing. In case you have difficulty picturing how long the 8.8m tapeworm actually is, the museum has a helpful rope right next to the tapeworm display case that you can unroll.

The museum is surprisingly popular with dating couples. You have to admit - it is a unique date spot.

If the 15-minute walk to the museum is too much, regular buses going in the direction of the museum leave from the West Exit of Meguro Station. Any bus, except number 09, will take you to bus stop Otori-Jinja-Mae, only a minute's walk from the Meguro Parasitological Museum.

Omotesando

 Tokyo Metro: Omotesando Station JR: Harajuku Station

 〒150-0001　東京都渋谷区神宮前4-30-3　東急プラザ表参道原宿 (Tokyu Plaza Omotesando, Jingu-mae 4-30-3, Shibuya-ku, Tokyo Postcode:150-0001)

 omohara.tokyu-plaza.com

 Most shops 11:00-21:00 & restaurants 11:00-23:00.

Omotesando is Harajuku grown up. The wide avenue, lined with striking zelkova trees and up-market fashion boutiques, stretches from Aoyama-dori to the entrance to Meiji Jingu Shrine.

The atmosphere, combined with its reputation as a fashion and design center and its stylish cafés lead it to be called the *Champs-*

Elysées of Tokyo. Every year, Omotesando hosts a St. Patrick's Day parade.

Omotesando is something of an architectural showcase, featuring cutting-edge designs from leading architects.

If you need a starting point, how about Tokyu Plaza Omotesando? The six-floor

mall describes itself as a shopping theme park, and is famous for its entranceway, made up of a dazzling array of mirrors.

The *omohara no mori* (forest plaza) on the sixth floor offers the chance to grab a coffee and relax beneath the trees while enjoying the view over the street below.

Shibuya Parco

 JR and Tokyo Metro: Shibuya Station

 〒150-0042 東京都渋谷区宇田川町１５–1
15-1 Udagawacho, Shibuya City, Tokyo 150-0042

 shibuya.parco.jp

 11:00-21:00

With no shortage of shopping and dining in this area, Shibuya Parco had to be radically different to become popular with locals when it opened in late 2019 - and it is!

This shopping center features Japan's first appetizer Store (with a Pokemon Center), a museum and gallery, a rooftop park on level 10, and *depachika* with quirky

food outlets designed to feel like you are in old alleyways.

Plus all the other shopping, of course!

Museum of Yebisu Beer

 JR and Tokyo Metro: Ebisu Station (5 mins)

 Entry price: Free/ Tours: 500 yen (includes 2 beers)

 〒153-0062 東京都目黒区三田4-20-1 恵比寿ガーデンプレイス内
Yebisu Garden Place, 4-20-1 Ebisu, Shibuya-ku, Tokyo Postcode:153-0062

 11:00-19:00 (Closed Monday)

 sapporoholdings.jp

To celebrate 120 years of brews, Yebisu opened the Museum of Yebisu Beer in 2007.

You can browse the gallery, comprising of old advertisements yourself, but joining a 40 minute guided tour is recommended. Although conducted in

Japanese, the tour includes the chance to sample some of Yebisu's products (soft drinks available). It concludes with a rock-paper-scissors tournament, with the winner receiving another beer in a souvenir glass.

The Museum of Yebisu Beer

is located within the Ebisu Garden Place, a beautiful mini city within a city built on the site of the former Yebisu brewery.

The brewery gave its name to the surrounding town and station. Yebisu is the old way of writing 'Ebisu'.

Meguro River

 JR, Tokyo Metro and Toei Subway: Meguro Station

 Free

 東京都目黒区上目黒 (Meguro, Meguro-ku, Tokyo)

 city.meguro.tokyo.jp

24 hours (cherry blossom season is late March/early April)

Meguro River is a concrete-lined canal that meanders through Meguro. It is not usually a draw, except in the spring when the 800 cherry trees that line the river burst into spectacular life.

A festival springs up around the cherry blossom, with food stalls lining the pleasant walkway. At night, the cherry blossoms are illuminated by 400,000 tiny LED lights.

From Meguro Station, walk downhill towards Yamate-dori (Yamate street), passing by the old-style stores selling cooking pots and pottery. Before long, you'll find yourself beside the river.

If you have time, Meguro River is best combined with a trip to the nearby Meguro Parasitological Museum (see page 51).

Eat

Mr. Chicken
Nearest Station: JR Lines: Osaki Station (12 mins)
Phone: 03-6687-9367
Address: 〒141-0041 東京都品川区北品川5-12-6 若林ビル103 (Wakabayashi-biru 103, Kita-Shinagawa 15-12-5, Shinagawa, Tokyo Postcode: 141-0041)
Hours: 11:30-14:00 and 18:00-23:00. Closed Sundays and national holidays.
Website: www.mrchicken.jp

This Singaporean street food classic developed by Hainanese immigrants features beautifully poached chicken served on a fragrant bed of jasmine rice steamed in chicken broth. It is aromatic and tasty.

Either dine in at Mr. Chicken's Shinagawa location, or grab a takeaway from their delivery truck which frequents Omotesando, Harajuku and Yurakucho during the lunch hour (details on their website). A standard serving of chicken rice costs ¥800.

Maisen Tonkatsu Aoyama Honten
Nearest Station: Tokyo Metro: Omotesando Station / JR Lines: Harajuku Station
Phone: 03-3470-0071
Address: 〒150-0001 東京都渋谷区 神宮前4-8-5 (4-8-5 Jingumae, Shibuya-ku, Tokyo, Japan)
Hours: 11:00-20:00
Website: mai-sen.com

Tonkatsu is a deep-fried pork cutlet, with a crispy outer coating of bread crumbs that perfectly complements the succulent meat within. It is generally served on rice with a side of thinly sliced raw cabbage, or with Japanese-style curry (more like a stew than Indian curry). Maisen is considered one of the best *tonkatsu* in Japan.

The restaurant has been serving *tonkatsu* since 1965 and is located within a former public bathhouse, traces of which remain in the architecture. Maisen is popular and there is often a queue for seats. There's also a takeout counter.

A set menu costs ¥3,100, or ¥2,600 for the tonkatsu only.

Maidreamin Shibuya Cafe & Dining Bar
Nearest Station: JR Lines/ Tokyo Metro: Shibuya Station
Phone: 03-6272-3263
Address: 〒150-0042 東京都渋谷区宇田川町30-1 蓬莱屋ビルB1 (Horaiya BLDG.B1F,30-1 Udagawacho Shibuya -ku Tokyo 150-8010)
Hours: 11:30-23:00

Website: maidreamin.com

Maid cafés are a well known Japanese phenomenon. There are a ton across Tokyo, ranging from decidedly cute to decidedly sleazy.

If you want to experience a maid cafe without the uncomfortable vibes, try Maidreamin's chain of maid cafés across Tokyo.

The Shibuya location, located away from geek hotspots, has a nice atmosphere. Strict rules against photographing the interior and staff (it's okay to photograph your food) cut down on the creep factor.

The food is cute, decorated for you by your waitress. You have the same waitress throughout your visit, and she will be friendly, inviting you to join her in games and conversation. In addition to the food, there is a cover charge of ¥500 per hour.

Maidreamin offers meal sets. For example, a meal of *omuraisu*, a drink and a photo with your waitress comes to ¥2,500.

Hakushu Teppanyaki
Nearest Station: JR Lines/ Tokyo Metro: Shibuya Station (5 mins)
Phone: 03-3461-0546

Address: 〒150-0031 東京都 渋谷 桜丘町 17-10 MCD Building 1F (17-10 Sakuragaokacho | 1F MCD Bldg., Shibuya 150-0031, Tokyo)
Hours: Monday-Saturday: 17:30-23:00, (closed Sundays and National holidays)

Website: hakushu-tokyo.business.site/

Teppan-yaki is another must-try while in Tokyo. It is the practice of cooking on an iron grill in front of the customers, and it makes for an exciting dining experience, with food arriving fresh off the grill, prepared to the customer's specifications (if you are brave enough to tell the chef how you prefer your steak!).

Hakushu in Shibuya offers delectable Kobe steak, grilled to perfection, in a cozy venue. The family-run restaurant has been serving happy customers for over fifty years. It has only twenty seats, making reservations essential. Dinner starts around ¥5,000.

Stay

Dormy Inn Premium Shibuya Jingumae Hot Spring
Nearest Station: Tokyo Metro: Meiji Jingu Mae 'Harajuku' Station / JR Lines: Harajuku Station
Phone: 03-5774-5489
Address: 〒 1 5 1 - 8 5 5 7　東京都渋谷区神宮前 6 - 2 4 - 4 (6-24-4 Jingumae, Shibuya-ku, Tokyo, 150-0001, Japan)
Website: dormyinn-shibuya-jingumae.h-rez.com

Located in Yoyogi, walking distance from Meiji Jingu Shrine, Yoyogi Park, and the shopping districts Harajuku and Omotesando, this is a 3-star hotel with fantastic amenities.

Electric bikes are available to rent, and multi-lingual staff is on hand to assist if needed. There is a free and frequent shuttle bus to Shibuya Station.

Rooms start around ¥14,000 including breakfast.

A western-style bathroom is attached to each room, but you'd be remiss if you don't try out the hotel's onsen, the hot spring referred to in the hotel's name.

Keiunso Ryokan
Nearest Station: JR Lines / Tokyo Metro: Shinjuku Station
Phone: 03-3370-0333
Address: 〒 1 5 1 - 8 5 5 7　東京都渋谷区代々 木 2 - 4 - 2 (2-4-2 Yoyogi, Shibuya-ku, Tokyo Postcode:151-0053)
Website: keiunso.hotels-tokyo-jp.com

Keiunso Ryokan is a small 2-star Japanese style Inn located in Yoyogi, conveniently close to Shibuya and Shinjuku. The 24-room hotel sleeps its guests on traditional futon, laid out on tatami mats. This is surprisingly comfortable, and visitors who prefer a harder mattress may actually find they prefer it.

Unfortunately, Keiunso has a strict schedule. Check-in begins at 16:00 and guests must be out of their rooms by 10:00 for cleaning. The 24:00 curfew may be inconvenient for guests planning to take advantage of Shinjuku and Shibuya's vibrant nightlife.

What Keiunso lacks in convenience, they make up for in price. Single rooms start at around ¥6,000, with doubles from ¥10,000.

Taito

Taito is the smallest of Tokyo's wards, but it is packed with important sites, from Senso-ji, Tokyo's oldest and liveliest temple, to Ueno Park, Japan's first public park and the location of a decisive battle between supporters of Emperor Meiji and the fading shogunate. Even the shopping arcades have a retro feel: Taito offers visitors an insight into the bustle and buzz of Tokyo's lively past.

See and Do

Asakusa Culture Tourist Information Center

 Tokyo Metro, Toei Asakusa Line, Tobu Isesaki Line and Tsukuba Express: Asakusa Station

 Free

 東京都台東区雷門 2－1 8－9 (2-18-9 Kaminarimon, Taito-ku, Tokyo)

 city.taito.lg.jp

 09:00-20:00

The Asakusa Culture Tourist Information Center is almost a tourist attraction in itself.

The center is housed in a beautiful modern building, designed by Kengo Kuma. It is comprised not of stories, but of eight one floor houses stacked on top of each other. This makes for a unique design, held together by the architect's skillful use of cohesive building elements. The building is a lively addition to Asakusa's bustling atmosphere.

Inside, the staff at the Tourist Information Center are available to assist tourists with a variety of queries. They speak English, Chinese and Korean.

Free Wi-Fi is available and there are a few internet PCs. There are public bathrooms and a few restaurants within the building, making it a good place to relax while you plot your next adventure.

On the eighth floor, the terrace observatory gives good views over surrounding Asakusa.

Tokyo National Museum

 JR: Uguisudani Station
JR & Tokyo Metro : Ueno Station (12 mins)

 1,000 yen. The Kuroda Memorial Hall is free.

 〒110-8712　東京都台東区上野公園13-9　東京国立博物館 (13-9 Ueno Park, Taito-ku, Tokyo, 110-8712, Japan)

 tnm.jp

⊘ 9:30-17:00. Closed Mon. When Mon is a holiday, the museum opens Mon & closes on the next day.

Founded in 1872, Tokyo National Museum houses the biggest collection of Japanese art - including kimono, Buddhist sculpture, bowls and vases, woodcut, decorated screens and scrolls - in the world. With 110,000 items, the museum frequently rotates its displays, making the museum worth a repeat visit.

In addition to the Japanese art, housed in the Honkan, the museum has some interesting additional buildings. The Hyokeikan, built in 1909 to commemorate the Taisho Emperor's wedding, is an excellent example of Meiji period architecture, and houses temporary exhibitions.

The Heiseikan, houses exhibits relating to Ancient Japan.

The Toyokan, built in 1968, houses Asian art, in particular Chinese, Korean, Indian and Egyptian art and artifacts.

The newest addition to the Museum is the Horyuji Homotsukan, built to house religious treasures donated by Nara's Horyuji temple. Finally, the Kuroda Memorial Hall has displays of Kuroda Seiki's paintings (known as the father of modern Western style art in Japan).

There is more to take in here than most tourist itineraries allow for.

Spend a few hours on the Honkan's collection, before heading over to browse the Horyuji Homotsukan. Then refresh yourself with a coffee and a bite in one of the museum's many cafés, or, in spring and autumn, head to the tea house in the gardens for a more traditional pick me up. From there, you can continue to browse the museum's collections, or head off to another of Ueno's many attractions.

On Museum Day, May 19th, and Respect for the Aged Day (third Monday in September) admission is free.

Senso-ji

 Tobu Skytree, Tokyo Metro and Tsukuba Express Line: Asakusa Station Toei Subway: Toei Asakusa Station

 Free, but donations are welcome.

 〒111-0032 東京都 台東区浅草2-3-1 (2-3-1 Asakusa, Taito-ku, Tokyo Postcode: 111-0032)

 senso-ji.jp

🕐 06:00-17:00 (Oct-March 06:30-17:00)

Senso-ji predates Tokyo, being founded in 645. When two brothers fished a beautiful statue of Kannon from the Sumida River, Tokyo was still a tiny fishing village - much like the village of Asakusa, where the brothers took their find.

The village headman recognized the value of the statue and converted his house into a shrine for it, the first incarnation of Senso-ji temple.

A visiting Buddhist priest, the first of many pilgrims, directed the statue to be concealed from the public, and a proper temple built. Senso-ji's popularity grew and grew—as did Tokyo.

As Edo expanded outwards, absorbing Asakusa into the growing city, Tokugawa Ieyasu made Senso-ji his family temple.

Visiting Senso-ji is like stepping back in time. As you step through the distinctive Kaminarimon (Thunder Gate) with its outsize lanterns and grimacing guardian statues, you are greeted by the same sight tourists have seen for centuries: rows of stalls selling souvenirs, temple goods and snacks.

Senso-ji's shopping street offers a mix of traditional snacks and modern additions. The souvenirs tend to be over-priced, but the food is irresistible.

Before entering the Hon-do (main temple), purify yourself by waving smoke from the incense burning in the pots in front of the temple over yourself. Then, climb the steps. Not all of the temple is open to tourists, but enjoy what is.

Senso-ji has some beautiful artwork on the ceiling and walls. There is plenty to see, including a five-story pagoda and some lovely gardens. Pause a moment to take in the view over the temple grounds to the Tokyo skyline beyond.

On the grounds of Senso-ji is Asakusa-shrine, dedicated to the fishermen and village headman responsible for Senso-ji. It is located to the East of Senso-ji, through a great stone tori gate. The shrine survived WWII air-raids (unlike Senso-ji), making it one of the older shrines still within Tokyo.

It's worth visiting while you're at Senso-ji, if only for the example of how two religions can peacefully coexist. Senso-ji is a Buddhist temple, but its founders are enshrined in a Shinto shrine.

Ueno Park

 JR: Ueno Station
Keisei Lines: Keisei Ueno Station
Tokyo Metro: Ueno Station (5 mins)

 The park is free. Admission fee for the museums and the zoo.

 〒110-0007 東京都台東区上野公園５-２０ (Uenokoen, 5–20 Taito-ku, Tokyo Postcode: 110-0007)

 kensetsu.metro.tokyo.lg.jp/jimusho/toubuk/ueno/en_index.html

Museums 9:30-17:30. Closed Mondays.

Once the grounds of Kanei-ji Temple, Ueno Park became Japan's first public park following the Meiji Restoration. Kanei-ji Temple was a favorite of the shogunate, and so became a target for forces loyal to the Emperor.

Dotted around Ueno Park today are traces of the shogunate's 250-year rule. Toshogu Shrine is dedicated to Tokugawa Ieyasu.

While Kanei-ji Temple was badly damaged during the battle to end the shogun's rule, Toshogu Shrine is one of the best-preserved in Tokyo.

Today, Ueno Park has something for everyone. The expansive park grounds include multiple national museums, art museums and a zoo, as well as temples and shrines—not to mention the park itself.

In spring, Ueno Park attracts cherry blossom enthusiasts, while in the summer, Lake Biwako is home to blooming water lilies.

There's almost always something going on, as Ueno Park is a popular destination for buskers and food carts.

Shitamachi Museum

 JR and Tokyo Metro:
Ueno Station
Keisei Lines: Keisei
Ueno Station (5 mins)

 300 yen

 〒110-0007 台東区
上野公園2番1号
(Ueno-Koen 2-1,
Taito-ku, Tokyo
Postcode: 110-0007)

 uenotoshogu.com

 09:30-16:30. Closed
Mondays. When
Mon is a national
holiday, the museum
opens Mon and
closes the next day

While history books and other museums concentrate on the elite power players of history, the Shitamachi Museum is dedicated to the life of the common folk. Shitamachi was the name given to the district where Edo's merchants and laborers lived and worked—modern Taito and Sumida.

The museum's exhibits are intended to recreate life in the dangerously crowded confines in 1910-20 when the area experienced a time of growth and expansion.

The first floor has scale recreations of Taisho-era buildings, including a merchant's house, a row of apartments, and a blacksmith's workshop. Upstairs, you'll find smaller exhibits, including traditional toys.

The Shitamachi Museum Annex in nearby Yanaka is a free museum, in a building dating from 1910. It recreates the interior of a Meiji-era liquor store and is worth a visit too.

Tokyo Metropolitan Art Museum

 JR Lines and Tokyo Metro: Ueno Station (7 mins)
Keisei Line: Keisei Ueno Station (10 mins)

 Varies by exhibition, about 700 yen

 〒110-0007 東京都台東区上野公園8番36号
8-36 Ueno-Park Taito-ku, Tokyo 110-0007

Sun to Thurs 9:30-17:30, Fri & Sat 9:30-20:00. Closed every 1st and 3rd Monday. If Monday is a holiday, the museum opens Monday and closes on the next day.

tobikan.jp

The Tokyo Metropolitan Art Museum is a red-brick building that houses six separate galleries. The Museum Gallery is used for special exhibitions organized by the museum. Galleries 1-5 can be rented out by art groups.

As a result, the Museum hosts an ever-changing series of exhibits that vary wildly from visit to visit. Instruction and signage are minimalist, reflecting the buildings' design, but the galleries are crammed full of art. This is the place to come for contemporary Japanese art.

The museum has family days every 3rd Saturday and Sunday of the month when Tokyo residents with a child aged under 18 pay a reduced admission fee to special exhibits. Although not applicable to most tourists, its worth keeping in mind as the museum will likely be crowded at these times. On Silver days, the third Wednesday of the month, visitors over 65 years old, enter the special exhibits free of charge.

Ameyayokocho

 JR Lines and Tokyo Metro: Ueno Station
JR Lines: Okachimachi Station
Keisei Line: Keisei Ueno Station

 Free

 〒110-0005 東京都台東区上野6-10-7 (Ueno 6-10-7, Taito-ku, Tokyo Postcode: 110-0005)

 ameyoko.net

 Varies. Generally 10:00-20:00, closed Wednesdays.

Ameyayokocho, commonly abbreviated to Ameyoko, is an open-air street market from Ueno Station to Okachimachi Station.

From Ueno Station, head for the big Yodobashi camera building. Ameyoko begins through the entranceway beside Yodobashi. Look for the distinctive sign.

The market is home to 180 shops, selling a variety of wares, including fresh fruit and vegetables, meat and seafood, clothing, wallets and watches.

The market sprung up during the American occupation post-WWII. The name 'ame' may mean candy, being a reference to the area's candy shops (sugar was scarce and highly prized in the post-war period). Or 'ame' could reference 'America,' and the area's past as a black market selling American goods.

Ameyoko's biggest attraction is the atmosphere. The retro vibe of the buildings calls to mind a Tokyo of decades past. The vendors call out to pedestrians, and the market becomes especially lively during the New Year period.

There is lots to see and taste, and you may come away with a one of a kind souvenir. Look out for Shimura Shoten, a tiny store almost dwarfed by its yellow signs, advertising its cheap chocolate.

The food court at the bottom of the Ameyoko Central Building is visited by professional chefs, drawn by its wide range of ingredients.

Yanaka

 JR, Keisei Main Line and Toei: Nippori Station
Tokyo Metro: Sendagi Station

 Free

 〒110-0001 東京都台東区谷中3-13-7 (Yanesen Tourist Information & Culture Center, Yanaka 3-13-7, Taitou-Ku Postcode: 110-0001)

 Shopping hours vary from store to store, but generally 09:00-18:00.

 ti-yanesen.jp

If you enjoyed the retro vibes of Ameyoko and loved the cluttered shopping street Kappabashi, then Yanaka is a must-visit.

This atmosphere of

Shitamachi lingers in this forgotten neighborhood of Tokyo, walking distance from Ueno Park and easily combined with a visit to one of Ueno's many museums.

Exiting Nippori station, you'll find Yanaka Cemetery to your left. During cherry blossom season, don't be surprised to find people having picnics within the cemetery grounds! At other times of years, the cemetery is good for a peaceful stroll.

You may find a couple of Yanaka's cat population dozing in the sun. The stray cats are encouraged by Yanaka's locals, and cat goods are prominently displayed in local shops.

Head to Yanaka Ginza, the area's main shopping street, to start your exploration. Many of the businesses are still family-run, with the proprietor living above the shop. New businesses, including a Western bakery and a T-shirt printing shop, stand side-by-side with the old. From traditional candy, to bamboo utensils, to a

range of cat-shaped goods, Yanaka reflects the needs of the people who live there. Sample Japanese-style pickles from the specialty pickle shop, or try *taiyaki*, a pancake-like concoction, shaped like a fish and stuffed with sweet red bean paste.

The buildings are shabby compared to Tokyo's glitzier neighborhoods, but that is part of its charm.

Many of the buildings have been repurposed. An old public bath is now SCAI, one of Tokyo's best-known art galleries, for example, and traditional houses remain on Yanaka's sidestreets.

The tourist information center sells English maps for ¥300. Guided tours of the neighborhood are also available, or simply stroll through the area, and see what you discover.

Yanaka offers the chance to witness traditional craftsmen, such as tatami-makers, going about their everyday work. If you want to try your hand at them you can.

The information center will help you reserve calligraphy, soba-making (buckwheat noodles), and pottery workshops, as well as cooking and Japanese language lessons.

Toshogu Shrine

 JR and Tokyo Metro: Ueno Station
Keisei Lines: Keisei Ueno Station

 Grounds: Free. Inside: 500 yen

 〒110-0007 東京都台東区上野公園9-88 (9-88 Ueno Koen, Taito-ku, Tokyo)

 uenotoshogu.com

October-February: 9:00-16:30, March-Sep: 9:00-17:30.

Toshogu Shrine is one of the best-preserved of Ueno's temples. Toshogu shrine was founded in 1627, and extensively rebuilt under the direction of Ieyasu's ambitious grandson, Iemitsu in 1651. It demonstrates not only the wealth and power of the Tokugawa shoguns but the architectural style representative of the Edo-period.

Of particular interest is the Sukibei wall, built in 1651, a

colorful wall that surrounds the shrine building. It is beautifully carved and painted in the style of the Edo-period.

The Karamon, a Chinese style gate decorated with gold foil, also dates from 1651. According to legend the two dragons on this gate leave every night to drink in the nearby pond.

The inside of the shrine is closed to visitors, but you

can walk around the outside, admiring the gold foil and detailed carvings.

The peony garden is open from January 1st to mid-February and mid-April to mid-May. Admission is ¥700. The garden was founded in 1980 to promote harmonious relationships between Japan and China. The peony was introduced to Japan from China, and achieved special prominence in the Edo period.

Eat

Asakusa Kagetsudo Honten
Nearest Station: Tobu Skytree Line/Tokyo Metro/Tsukuba Express Line: Asakusa Station (5 mins) / Toei Subway: Toei Asakusa Station (7 mins)
Phone: 03-3847-5251
Address: 東京都台東区浅草2－2－10 (Asakusa 2-2-10 Taito-ku Tokyo)
Hours: 09:00-17:00
Website: asakusa-kagetudo.com

Melon-pan is a staple of convenience stores and bakeries. 'Pan' is the Japanese word for bread and melon-pan a sweet bun scored at the top to resemble a sliced melon.

Today's melon-pan generally has some form of artificial melon flavoring, but Asakusa Kagetsudo makes theirs the old-fashioned way, with milk and butter.

Fresh from the oven and topped with crystalized sugar, the bread is the perfect combination of crunchy crust and soft interior. One jumbo-sized melon-pan is ¥220. The store also sells old-fashioned soft drinks and some Japanese-style desserts.

Tenya Asakusa Branch
Nearest Station: Tokyo Metro: Tawaramachi Station / Toei Subway: Toei Asakusa Station (7 mins)
Phone: 03-5828-5918
Address: 〒111-0032 東京都台東区浅草1-9-1 国立ビル (Kunitachi Building, 1-9-1 Asakusa Taito-ku, Tokyo Postcode:111-0032)
Hours: Mon-Fri 11:00-23:00, Sat and Sun/Holidays: 10:00-23:00
Website: tenya.co.jp

Tempura is a variation on a Portuguese recipe that has become a Japanese staple. It consists of thinly sliced vegetables and seafood, fried in a light batter and served either in bowls of broth with tasty *soba* (buckwheat noodles) or *udon* (thick wheat noodles).

If you want tasty tempura without spending a fortune, Tenya is a chain store with quality meals at great prices. The Classic One Coin Tendon gives you five pieces of tempura on rice for ¥500. Tenya offers vegetarian sets, as well as the option of udon and soba.

Waentei-Kikko
Nearest Station: Tobu Skytree Line/Tokyo Metro/Tsukuba Express Line: Asakusa Station / Toei Subway: Toei Asakusa Station
Phone: 03-5828-8833
Address: 〒111-0032 東京都台東区浅草2-2-13 (2-2-13 Asakusa Taito-ku, Tokyo)
Hours: 11:30-13:30, 17:30-21:00. Closed Wed.
Website: waentei-kikko.com

Waentei-Kikko is a Japanese restaurant focused on capturing the three meanings of 'en'—celebration, forming human bonds, and musical performance.

The last is provided by the proprietor, Fukui Kodai, an accomplished shamisen player. The shamisen is often described as a Japanese guitar. Its delicate sounds are the perfect accompaniment to your traditional meal, while the restaurant's understated decoration, reminiscent of an Edo-period farmhouse, further enhances the restaurant's unique ambiance.

Lunch is either a 1-layer *bento* (traditional Japanese lunch box) for ¥2,500 or 2-layer *bento* for ¥3,500. Both *bento* contain nine items.

Dinner consists of five different courses from ¥6,800, with two special course menus including *fugu*, the infamous poisonous blowfish, which is a delicacy from ¥9,800.

Sometaro Okonomiyaki
Nearest Station: Tokyo Metro: Tawaramachi Station
Phone: 03-3844-9502
Address: 〒111-0035 東京都台東区西浅草2-2-2 (2-2-2 Nishiasakusa, Taito-ku, Tokyo)
Hours: 12:00-20:15. Closed Tuesdays.

Okonomiyaki is described variously as a savory pancake or Japanese style pizza. It is a batter of thinly sliced cabbage combined with the ingredients of the customer's choosing (*okonomiyaki* roughly translates to 'cooked as you like'), cooked on a metal grill and then topped with *bonito* (dried tuna) flakes, *okonomiyaki* sauce, mayonnaise and *nori* (seaweed) flakes.

Located within the Kappabashi shopping area, the shop has a distinctively old-time vibe. The original building was lost to WWII air-raids, but it is lovingly recreated with Showa era posters and furnishings.

A basic okonomiyaki starts at ¥500. You cook your own okonomiyaki. The friendly staff, used to foreigners, will help you as needed.

Komagata Dozeu Asakusa
Nearest Station: Toei Subway: Kuramae Station
Phone: 03-3842-4001
Address: 東京都台東区駒形 1-7-12 (Komagata1-7-12, Taito-ku, Tokyo)
Hours: 11:00-21:00
Website: dozeu.com

Komagata Dozeu invites customers to "experience the taste of Edo." The restaurant has been in business for over 200 years.

The traditional building, built during the Edo period, is lovingly maintained. Each floor has a different atmosphere. Kimono-clad waitresses serve the restaurant's specialty—*dojo nabe*, a hot pot meal you cook yourself on a charcoal grill set up on your table.

Dojo is a freshwater loach, traditionally popular among the Edo-working class as a cheaper alternative to eel. As your *dojo* cooks, add as much or as little of the thinly sliced spring onions to your pot and eat as soon as you deem them ready. Season with some shichimi pepper and you're ready to eat. *Dojo nabe* starts at ¥1,750. Unlike most hot-pot meals, these come as single servings.

Stay

Khaosan World Asakusa
Nearest Station: Tsukuba Express: Tsukuba Asakusa Station / Tokyo Metro: Tawaramachi Station (8 mins) / Tobu Skytree Line/ Tokyo Metro/Tsukuba Express Line: Asakusa Station 11 mins) / Toei Subway: Toei Asakusa Station (13 mins)
Phone: 03-3843-0153
Address: 東京都台東区西 浅草3-15-1　カオサンワ ールド浅草 旅館/ホステル (3-15-1 NishiAsakusa, Taito-ku, Tokyo)
Website: khaosan-tokyo.com/en/

Khaosan World Asakusa is located within a former love hotel, and offers a range of accommodation options, including mixed and female-only dormitory rooms, Japanese style group rooms, and double rooms.

There is a shared kitchen, a dining room, a reading room stocked with comics and an information lounge. The staff has excellent English.

There are frequent live events including jazz performances every Thursday. A single bed in the dormitory starts at ¥3,200 at this 2-star hostel.

Toukaisou Ryokan/Hostel
Nearest Station: Tsukuba Express: Tsukuba Asakusa Station (4 mins) / Tokyo Metro: Tawaramachi Station (5 mins) / Tobu Skytree Line/Tokyo Metro/ Tsukuba Express Line: Asakusa Station (13 mins) / Toei Subway: Toei Asakusa Station (13 mins)
Phone: 03-3844-5618
Address: 〒111-0035 東京 都台東区西浅草2-16-12 浅 草旅館 東海荘 (2-16-12 Nishiasakusa Taitou-Ku Tokyo)
Website: toukaisou.com

Toukaisou is a combination of ryokan and hostel. The 2-star rooms on the first and second floor, are Japanese-style with a Western-style mattress and come with a private bathroom.

The rates start at ¥4,500 for a single room. The third floor offers dormitory-style bunk beds. You have the option of a bed in the mixed dormitory ¥2,700 per night, or a private dormitory for groups from 2-5 people, ¥3,000 per night).

Toukaisou has a small kitchenette, but no real cooking facilities, although there are plenty of shops and supermarkets nearby for a cheap meal.

Red Planet Hotels Asakusa
Nearest Station: Tsukuba Express: Tsukuba Asakusa Station / Tokyo Metro: Tawaramachi Station (5 mins) / Tobu Skytree Line/ Tokyo Metro/Tsukuba Express Line: Asakusa Station 8 mins) / Toei Subway: Toei Asakusa Station (10 mins)
Phone: 03-5828-0177
Address: 〒111-0032東京 都台東区浅草1-11-6 (1-11-6 Asakusa, Taito-ku Tokyo Postcode: 111-0032)
Website: redplanethotels.com

Red Planet Hotels claims to offer a 3-star hotel experience that is full of value without any hidden costs. The cheapest single room is about ¥7,000 after tax, which is good value for a hotel room in Tokyo.

Breakfast is another ¥1,000, but all other amenities Red Planet Hotel offers are free.

Sumida

Sumida is bounded on two sides by rivers, the Sumida river which gives the district its name, and the Arakawa river. Along with neighboring Taito, Sumida is what remains of Shitamachi where during the Edo-period, merchants, craftsmen, fishermen and laborers lived. Today, Sumida's historic legacy continues with the Edo-Tokyo Museum and sumo stables.

See and Do

Tokyo Skytree

 Tokyo Metro, Toei Asakusa Line, Narita Sky Access Keisei Line: Oshiage Station (5 mins)
Skytree Line: Tokyo Skytree Station

 See description

 〒131-0045 東京都 墨田区押上1-1-2 (1-1-2 Oshiage, Sumida, Tokyo Postcode: 131-0045)

 tokyo-skytree.jp

 08:00-22:00

The Skytree offers the best views over Tokyo with two viewing platforms, the 350m tembo deck and 450m galleria. On a clear day, the view over Tokyo extends all the way to Mt. Fuji.

The view from the Skytree is beautiful at day or night. Try and time your visit for late afternoon to get the best of both worlds. Enjoy a meal or a snack in one of the Skytree's many restaurants or bars as you wait for Tokyo to light up.

As well as the viewing platforms, the Skytree houses an aquarium, theater, commercial facilities and an exhibition center. Its also fast becoming a tourist hub.

Since its opening in 2012, the Skytree has been a popular draw for foreign and domestic visitors.

Expect long lines, and reserve tickets ahead of time when possible.

A Skytree Fast ticket for International Visitors (shorter queues) is ¥3,200 for access to the 350m tembo deck, ¥4,200 for tembo deck and 450m galleria. Regular tickets are ¥2,100 for the tembo deck, and a further ¥1,000 for the galleria.

Solamachi

Tobu Skytree Line: Tokyo Skytree Station
Tokyo Metro, Toei and Narita Sky Access Keisei Line: Oshiage
Station (5 mins)

〒131-0045 東京都墨田区押上1-1-2
1-1-2 Oshiage, Sumida, Tokyo Postcode: 131-0045

10:00-21:00 (6F 7F 30F 31F restaurants open 11:00-23:00)

 Free

 tokyo-solamachi.jp

Tokyo Solamachi is the huge shopping mall complex at the base of the Skytree.

Its 300 shops include an entire floor aimed at tourists with unique stores including character goods, Japanese interior design items, snacks and other souvenirs. It also has four floors of restaurants and big Japanese brands like Uniqlo.

The building is new, and worth exploring, even if you're only there to window shop.

The Solamachi complex also houses the Konica Minolta Planetarium Tenku, which offers visitors the chance to combine aromatherapy with audiovisual shows of the night sky from ¥1,500.

Sumida Aquarium

Tokyo Metro, Toei and Narita Sky Access Keisei Line:
Oshiage Station (5 mins)
Tobu Skytree Line: Tokyo Skytree Station

5-6F SOLAMACHI 〒131-0045 東京都墨田区押上1-1-2 (5-6F Solamachi 1-1-2
Oshiage, Sumida, Tokyo Postcode: 131-0045)

09:00-21:00 (last entry 20:00)

 2,300 yen

 tokyo-solamachi.j

The Sumida Aquarium is one of the Skytree complex's main attractions. Located within the Solamachi mall, the aquarium houses over 10,000 sea creatures.

The centerpiece of the aquarium is the 350,000-liter tank, home to dozens of penguins and fur seals.

The tank is designed without visible supports so that visitors have an uninterrupted view of the tank's occupants.

The aquarium is lit with environmentally-friendly LED lights that mimic the natural daylight levels, dimming as the afternoon progresses so the animals can enjoy as close to natural living conditions as possible.

Other highlights include the backlit jellyfish displays, showcasing the delicacy of these unlikely beauties, and tanks recreating water environments around Tokyo, and the Izu and Ogasawara Islands.

The aquarium also houses a research laboratory.

Sumida Hokusai Museum

 Toei Subway: Ryogoku Station (5 mins)
JR: Ryogoku Station (9 mins)

 〒130-0014 東京都墨田区亀沢2丁目7番2号
130-0014 2-7-2 Kamezawa, Sumida-ku, Tokyo

 09:30-17:30 (last entry 17:00). Closed Mondays and Dec 29-Jan 1. When Monday is a national holiday, the museum is open and closes the following day.

 400 yen

hokusai-museum.jp

Katsuhika Hokusai, known simply as Hokusai, is the master of ukiyo-e, the Edo-period woodcuts that charmed Tokyo's residents, intrigued the Western world, and influenced the art nouveau movement.

Hokusai's artwork is instantly recognizable. The famous image of Mt. Fuji framed between two perfectly stylized waves is part of Hokusai's series of views of Mt. Fuji. music

The Sumida Hokusai museum commemorates Hokusai's life.

He was born in Sumida, and the museum tries to recreate what life in Sumida would have been like 1760-1849, during Hokusai's life. It also houses a collection of Hokusai's woodcuts and a reconstruction of his studio.

Edo-Tokyo Museum

 Toei Subway and JR: Ryogoku Station

 600 yen

 〒130-0015 東京都墨田区横網1-4-1 (1-4-1 Yokoami, Sumida, Tokyo Postcode:130-0015)

edo-tokyo-museum.or.jp

09:30-17:30 (Saturdays 09:30-19:30), Closed Mondays unless it is a public holiday

The Edo-Tokyo Museum sheds vivid light on Sumida's past.

You enter the museum by crossing a full-size recreation of the Nihombashi bridge, the entry point into Edo for centuries of travelers, and from there continue into the city itself.

The museum's lifesize recreations of shops, houses and even a Kabuki theater allow you to easily imagine what life was like in Edo's downtown.

Tiny scale models, with loving and intricate detail, allow you to understand the sheer scale of Edo, evoking the crowded streets and precariously close houses in a way that no amount of ukiyo-e (traditional woodcuts popular in the Edo era) or history books can.

The museum's collection extends beyond the Edo-period, with Meiji-era and post-war items on display. There is excellent English-language information provided, and guided tours in English are also available. Ask at the ticket desk, or book in advance online.

Finally, the museum building itself is worth seeing. The futuristic building is a modern take on the traditional storehouses adopted by Edo-period residents in an effort to thwart the city's frequent fires.

Ryogoku Kokugikan (Sumo Stadium)

 Toei Subway and JR: Ryogoku Station

 See description. Museum: Free

 東京都墨田区横網1丁目3-28 (1-3-28 Yokoduna, Sumida-ku, Tokyo)

🌐 sumo.pia.jp

🕐 Museum Hours: 10:00-16:30. Closed weekends and public holidays, and match days for non-ticketholders.

Sumo is Japan's national sport, and Ryogoku Kokugikan is the site where three of the six official sumo tournaments take place in January, May and September.

The Ryogoku Kokugikan was built in 1985, and in addition to the stadium with a capacity of 11,000 people, houses a sumo museum. The area, Ryogoku, where the stadium is located, has been a sumo training ground for centuries.

The streets around the stadium are packed with sumo training schools, known as stables, and restaurants serving the hot-pot dishes beloved by the sumo wrestlers. It's worth a visit, even if there's not a match on.

Watching a sumo match should be high on the must-see list for every visitor to Japan. Don't worry if you don't understand the sport.

Sumo evolved as a Shinto religious rite, and is full of spectacle and ritual.

Seats in the stadium come in three options. The ring-side seats (close enough that spectators can be sprayed with sand) and boxes are incredibly popular and sell out fast. Still, the chair seats are far enough from the stage that you can eat or drink freely. Eating a bento while cheering on your wrestler of choice will make you truly feel part of the crowd.

The tournaments start around 09:00, with bouts between the younger, less prominent wrestlers and end in the evening, with the masters.

Ringside seats cost around ¥15,000, while box seats range from ¥10,000-12,000 dependent on location. Chairs range from ¥3,100-10,000. You can purchase tickets directly from the stadium on the day if you don't mind the risk of seats being filled. Otherwise, you can purchase tickets in advance online, by phone (0570-02-9999), or through conveniences stores.

Ryogoku Sumo Stables

 Toei Subway: Hamacho Station

 Free

 〒103-0007　東京都中央区日本橋浜町2-47-2
2-47-2, Hama-cho Nihonbashi Chuo-ku Tokyo

🕐 07:30-10:00

🌐 arashio.net

If you miss the sumo tournaments, don't despair! You can see genuine sumo in Sumida's Ryogoku district.

Ryogoku has been the home of sumo wrestling stables, known as *beya*, for centuries. Many sumo stables allow tourists to watch their morning practice sessions from a respectful distance or through a window. Some even offer tours. It's worth asking at your hotel for recommendations.

Arashio is among the most well-known stables open to visitors. The stable allows tourists to view the morning practice from a side-street through large windows.

There is room for about twelve people to stand and watch at one time.

There's no charge and no reservations, though it pays to call ahead and get confirmation of the time of the practice.

You can track down other stables that welcome visitors by looking at the Japan Sumo Association's list of stables or asking your hotel.

Most take holidays during March, July and November and are closed the week after the Grand tournament and at weekends.

Asahi Beer Hall

 Tokyo Metro: Asakusa station

 To enjoy the Sky Room you must make a purchase.

 〒131-0041 東京都墨田区 吾妻橋1-23-1 アサヒグループ本社ビル
Asahi Group Honsha-biru Azumabashi 1-23-1 Sumida-ku, Tokyo Postcode: 131-0041

🕐 Monday-Friday: 11:30-22:00 (closed 15:00-17:00), Saturday-Sunday: 11:30-16:00

 asahibeer.co.jp

Spend any time in Sumida, particularly around the river, and you can't help but notice a very distinctive building.

The golden sculpture on top of a squat black building has been confusing visitors to Tokyo ever since it was built in 1989. The building is the Asahi Beer Hall, and the golden object is known as the *flamme d'or* or golden flame, to represent the burning heart of Asahi beer. Tokyo residents say it resembles something else, nicknaming it the golden poo.

Next to the Asahi Beer Hall is the Asahi Breweries Headquarters, whose golden tint and textured top are designed to evoke a foaming mug of beer.

On the 22nd floor, the Sky Room offers the chance to sample Asahi beer while enjoying a beautiful over the city, including the nearby Skytree.

In an *izakaya*, Japanese pub, on the second floor, you can sample limited run Asahi craft beers.

Kyu Yasuda Teien Gardens

 Toei Subway and JR: Ryogoku Station

 Free

 〒130-0015 東京都墨田区横網１丁目１２−１ (Kyu-Yasuda Teien Gardens 1-12 Yokoami Sumida-ku Tokyo)

 bit.ly/kyuyasuda

 Apr to Sep 09:00-19:30, Oct to Mar 9:00-18:00

Kyu Yasuda Teien is a Japanese-style stroll garden north of the Ryogaku Kokugikan Sumo Stadium.

Once a samurai residence, the garden was famed for its pond which rose and fell with the tides of the nearby Sumida River.

The last private owner donated the land to the city of Tokyo on his death, but the Great Kanto earthquake destroyed the garden.

It was restored in 1927, only for the garden to be killed by the heavy levels of pollution in the river following Tokyo's post-war redevelopment. It was restored again in 1971.

Now the park makes a pleasant place to stroll. During the summer, evening tea-ceremonies and koto performances are held in the park, which attract street food vendors and copious mosquitoes. Invest in some repellent and enjoy the free entertainment.

Tobu Museum of Transport and Culture

 Tobu Isezaki Line: Higashi-mukojima Station

 200 yen

 東京都墨田区東駒島４−２８−１６
4-28-16 Higashi-mukojima, Sumida-ku, Tokyo

 10:00-16:30. Closed Mondays and Dec 29-Jan 3. When Monday is a national holiday, the museum opens and is closed the following day.

 tobu.co.jp/museum

The Tobu Museum is a must for railway and car enthusiasts.

The transport museum, maintained by the Tobu railway group, features twelve vintage vehicles, including Tobu's first steam locomotive, as well as train and bus driving simulations, a variety of model trains, and get close-up views of passing trains from a viewing area that takes advantage of the overhead railway tracks.

Unfortunately, the lack of English information makes this museum one for dedicated fans only.

Kanto Earthquake Memorial Museum

 JR and Toei Subway: Ryogoku Station (5 mins) Free

 東京都復興記念館 東京都墨田区横網2丁目3–5
2-3-5 Yokoami Sumida-ku Tokyo

 09:00-16:30. Closed Mondays. tokyoireikyoukai.or.jp

The Great Kanto Earthquake of 1923 devastated Tokyo. 70% of the city was lost to the quake and the fires that followed, and over 58,000 people lost their lives.

The Kanto Earthquake Memorial Museum is located on the grounds of the Tokyo Memorial Temple, commemorating all who died in the earthquake, as well as victims of war and other disasters.

The museum is small, with only two floors and limited English information. Make sure to get an English brochure to help you understand the exhibits.

The first floor shows the devastation following the earthquake, with maps showing the worst-hit areas, and twisted metal and glass demonstrating the intense heat of the resulting fires. On the second floor are diaries, artwork and school

work by local children and artists that show the personal impact of the earthquake on survivors.

Once finished with the museum, you can wander the grounds, paying your respects at the temple and pagoda. The temple is located on the site of the worst loss of life. Tragically, 38,000 people evacuated to this spot were trapped by the flames.

Tobacco and Salt Museum

 Tobu Skytree Line: Tokyo Skytree Station (8 mins)
Keikyu Line and Toei Subway: Honjo Azumabashi Station
Tokyo Metro, Toei and Narita Sky Access Keisei Line:
Oshiage Station (12 mins)

 Permanent exhibition: 100 yen, Special exhibition: 300 yen

 東京都墨田区横川町１–１６–３
1-16-3, Yokokawa, Sumida-ku Postcode:130-0003

 10:00-18:00 (Last entry 17:30). Closed Mondays and Dec 29-Jan 3. When Monday is a national holiday, the museum is open Monday and closed the following day.

 tabashio.jp

What do tobacco and salt have in common? Until recently, both were controlled by government monopolies in Japan. They're also both the subjects of the Tobacco and Salt Museum, built in 1978 by the government agency in charge of regulating them.

The museum explores the cultural, political and industry that salt and tobacco had on Japanese society.

The second floor explores the formation and production of salt within Japan and overseas, and includes equipment used to process salt on Japan's Noto

peninsula as well as a 1.4-ton piece of rock salt mined in Poland.

The third floor houses displays of smoking paraphernalia, including a reproduction of an Edo-period tobacco shop and an extensive collection of *ukiyo-e* (Japanese art) woodcuts.

Eat

Kapou Yoshiba

Nearest Station: Toei Subway: Ryogoku Station (6 mins)
Phone: 03-3623-4480
Address: 東京都墨田区横網2-14-5 (2-14-5 Yokoami, Sumida-ku, Tokyo)
Hours: 11:30-14:00, 17:00-22:00. Closed Sundays, national holidays, Golden Week, Obon and New Years.
Website: kapou-yoshiba.jp

Kapou Yoshiba is a truly one of a kind dining experience. The building was once a sumo stable, and Kapou Yoshiba has preserved the practice ring inside the restaurant. Once used by the Miyagino-beya wrestlers in practice, the ring is now used as a stage for traditional music performances.

Unsurprisingly, you can order the sumo staple, a *chanko-nabe*, hot pot dish packed with protein, here, starting at ¥5,600 for *chanko-nabe* for two.

Portions are sized appropriately for the sumo district, and Kapou Yoshiba is also known for its jumbo sushi and its lunchtime *nigiri* (hand-pressed sushi) set.

Moomin House Cafe

Nearest Station: Tobu Skytree Line: Tokyo Skytree Station / Tokyo Metro, Toei Subway and Narita Sky Access Keisei Line: Oshiage Station (5 mins)
Phone: 03-5610-3063
Address: 〒131-0045 東京都墨田区押上1-1-2 1F (1F 1-1-2 Oshiage, Sumida, Tokyo Postcode: 131-0045)
Hours: 8:00-22:30
Website: benelic.com

The Moomin House Cafe, located within the Solamachi mall at the base of the Skytree, is a character cafe inspired by the Finnish book and comics about the Moomins.

The interior has a quaint, European home style, further decorated with illustrations from the Moomin series. Large stuffed Moomin toys are placed around the cafe for customers to interact with.

The food is equally adorable, with Moomin shaped waffles, curry served with rice shaped into a Moomin head, and latte art featuring various characters.

Several menu items, such as the pancake stack or the souvenir silhouette latte come with an original character gift that you can take home with you.

If that's not enough Moomin for you, there is a store selling Moomin goods right next to the cafe. Breakfast starts at ¥700, lunch starts at ¥1,300, dinner starts at ¥1,800.

Rigoletto Rotisserie and Wine

Nearest Station: Tobu Skytree Line: Tokyo Skytree Station / Tokyo Metro, Toei Subway and Narita Sky Access Keisei Line: Oshiage Station (5 mins)
Phone: 03-5809-7401
Address: 〒131-0045 東京都墨田区押上1-1-2 2F ソラマチタワーヤード 2F (2F Tower Yard, Solamachi 1-1-2 Oshiage, Sumida, Tokyo Postcode: 131-0045)
Hours: 11:00-22:00
Website: rigoletto.jp

Rigoletto is a Spanish and Italian restaurant located within the Tokyo Skytree complex. It has an extensive menu with a variety of lunch sets, starting from the salad lunch, pizza lunch and pasta lunch from ¥900 each.

The dinner menu has an extensive range with pasta dishes starting from ¥900 yen, but with all the yummy tapas options (¥500 each), you'll struggle to stick to just one dish.

Toriton Tokyo Solamachi

Nearest Station: Tobu Skytree Line: Tokyo Skytree Station / Tokyo Metro, Toei Subway and Narita Sky Access Keisei Line: Oshiage Station (5 mins)
Phone: 03-5637-7716
Address: 〒131-0045 東京都墨田区押上1-1-2 2F ソラマチ6F (6F Solamachi 1-1-2 Oshiage, Sumida, Tokyo Postcode: 131-0045)
Hours: 11:00-22:00
Website: toriton-kita1.jp

Toriton is a *kaiten* (conveyor belt) sushi restaurant located in the Solamachi complex at the base of the SkyTree.

Toriton is instantly recognizable thanks to the long queues of people waiting. Fortunately, the queue moves quickly and the staff provides benches to sit on, so don't be put off the chance to sample one of the most fun ways to eat sushi.

Conveyor belt sushi is

generally cheaper and faster than eating sushi at a traditional sushi restaurant, though the quality may not be as good - but that's not an issue at Toriton.

Once a space becomes available, the staff will seat you at a place at the counter or a table (for groups of 4-6). The counter seats have less elbow room, but give you a better view of the sushi chefs at work. Take what you like from the conveyor belt, or order directly from the chef.

There is an English translation of the menu available on request. Hold up your fingers to indicate how many plates of each type of sushi you'd like. At the end, when you want your bill say '*gokaikei*'.

A meal here comes to between ¥1000-2000, depending on how extravagant you are with your sushi choices.

Stay

Hotel MYSTAYS Asakusa
Nearest Station: Toei Subway: Kurumae Station
Phone: 03-3626-2443
Address: 〒130-0004 東京都墨田区本所1-21-11 (1-21-11 Honjo, Sumida-ku, Tokyo 130-0004)
Website: mystays.com

Hotel MYSTAYS is a 2-star Western-style hotel with great views of the Tokyo Skytree, particularly if you book one of their Skytree-view rooms. Rooms start at ¥7,480 per night for one person in the cheapest available room (breakfast not included). Hotel MYSTAYS has an Indian restaurant, Doli, and every room includes a kitchenette.

Tsuruya Ryokan
Nearest Station: Tokyo Metro: Asakusa Station
Phone: 03-3622-9819
Address: 〒130-0001 東京都墨田区吾妻橋２－１８－２ (2-18-2 Azumabashi Sumida-ku Tokyo Japan)
Website: ne.jp/asahi/tsuruya/tokyo/

Tsuruya Ryokan is a 2-star Japanese style inn for those on a budget. Rooms start at ¥5,350 for a C-type room, 6 tatami mats in size with a toilet attached, or ¥5,880 for a 'D-type' room of the same size but with a shower and toilet. A-type rooms are twice the size, and come with a bath for ¥6,720 for one person.

Breakfast is Japanese style with bread and costs an additional ¥730, and dinner starts at ¥1,500 (price varies according to the seasonal menu). Breakfast and dinner must be arranged in advance. Tsuruya offers Japanese style hospitality at a reduced rate.

Communication can be an issue as the staff doesn't speak much English, but you can get help making reservations from Tokyo's many tourist information centers.

Ryogoku View Hotel
Nearest Station: JR and Toei Subway: Ryogoku Station
Phone: 03-3631-8111
Address: 〒130-0026 東京都墨田区両国 2-19-1 (2-19-1 Ryogoku, Sumida-ku, Tokyo Postcode 130-0026)
Website: viewhotels.co.jp/ryogoku/

If you are in Tokyo for the sumo, the 3-star Ryogoku View Hotel, with views over the sumo stadium, is a smart choice. Rooms start at ¥8,600 for a standard single room, ¥9,600 for the same room with breakfast. Due to its location, prices increase during the sumo tournaments.

There are a few different room types. The double-decker room features bunk beds, for example.

Furnishings are modern and colorful, with *ukiyo-e* inspired paintings giving a nod to the hotel's location.

The hotel has two restaurants and serves *chanko-nabe*, the hotpot dish loved by sumo wrestlers.

Further Afield and Day Trips

The areas outside the city's core contain some unique and fascinating places to explore, so be sure to include a day trip outside Tokyo during your stay.

Tokyo Disney Resort

 JR: Maihama Station

 1 day pass: 8,200 yen, Evening pass: 4,700 yen.

 〒279-8511 千葉県浦安市舞浜1番地1 (1-1 Maihama, Urayasu-shi, Chiba-ken)

 tokyodisneyresort.jp

Varies. Peak hours: 8:00-22:00, Off-peak: 8:00-19:00.

Tokyo Disneyland opened in 1983, the first Disneyland to be built outside the United States. It is modeled after Disneyland California and the Magic Kingdom Florida.

Many of Tokyo Disneyland's themed-areas and attractions closely resemble or duplicate those of the original Disney theme parks. It is a fun day out for families or for fans of theme parks, offering rides, performances, seasonal attractions, parades, themed restaurants, hotels and the ability to purchase an overwhelming amount of Disney goods.

Tokyo DisneySea is the second of the resort's theme park and incorporates characters and settings from more recent Disney movies such as Aladdin and The Little Mermaid, with classic literature, Jules Vernes' Journey to the Center of the Earth, and beautiful recreations of European architecture. The various 'ports of call' are linked by the theme of water. It is a beautiful theme park.

The resort attracts large crowds, resulting in extremely long waiting times for the more popular attractions. Tickets can be purchased in advance online, printed and presented at the park gates, meaning that you can enter Tokyo Disneyland Resort without waiting - tickets sell out in advance for peak date. Avoid weekends and holidays when crowds are extremely large.

As well as the train option, there are also direct buses to the Tokyo Disneyland resort from Narita Airport, Haneda Airport, Akihabara, and Yokohama stations.

If you are visiting Tokyo Disney Resort, take a look at our fantastic guide to make the most of your visit, *The Independent Guide to Tokyo Disney Resort*. It is available in both print and digital editions.

Studio Ghibli Museum

 JR Mitaka Station

 1000 yen

 〒181-0013 東京都
三鷹市下連雀1-1-
83 三鷹の森ジブ
リ美術館ＨＰ係 (1-
1-83 Shimorenjaku,
Mitaka, Tokyo
Postcode: 181-0013)

 ghibli-museum.jp

 At set times from
10:00 to 16:00.
Closed Tuesday.

The Studio Ghibli Museum, known officially as the Forest of Mitaka Ghibli Art Museum, is a museum and gallery dedicated to the art and characters of the animated movies produced by Hayao Miyazaki, and his Studio Ghibli film company.

The unique design of the museum building reflects the buildings within Studio Ghibli's films and is intended to immerse visitors in the world of the Ghibli movies. On display are animation cells and paintings produced for the movies, character models, a full-size reproduction of the original animation studio, and interactive displays such as a life-size Cat-bus, from My Neighbor Totoro, for children to play on.

The museum is small and very popular with domestic and foreign visitors, making advance reservations essential. Foreign visitors can buy tickets four months in advance through designated JTB outlets, spread throughout Asia, Europe, North America and Oceania. The Museum website has more details.

If you are already in Japan, tickets can be purchased a month ahead through Lawson convenience stores.

Mitaka is a suburb of Tokyo, 26 minutes by rapid train from Tokyo Station (¥390). From Mitaka Station South Exit, shuttle buses instantly recognizable by their Ghibli character designs carry you to the museum in 5 minutes for ¥210 one way, ¥320 return. Alternatively, it is a 15 to 20-minute walk through Inokashira Park.

Toshima Kuritsu Tokiwaso Manga Museum

 Toei Subway: Ochiai-minami-nagasaki Station (4 mins)
Seibu Ikebukuro Line: Shiinamachi Station (14 mins)

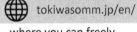 Free

 〒171-0052 東京都豊島区南長崎3丁目9–22
3 Chome-9-22 Minaminagasaki, Toshima City, Tokyo 171-0052, Japan

 10:00-18:00. Closed Mondays.

 tokiwasomm.jp/en/

Tokiwaso is a legendary apartment building where great modern manga artists including Tezuka Osamu lived together and spent their youth.

The original Tokiwaso was demolished in December 1982, but it was rebuilt as a manga museum that opened in July 2020.

The museum includes a recreation of the apartment building, a 'manga lounge' where you can freely browse the works of manga artists related to Tokiwaso, and am exhibition room where exhibitions and events are held. This is a must-do for manga fans!

Yokohama

Yokohama is the second biggest city in Japan, and it is so close to Tokyo that it is hard to tell where Tokyo ends and Yokohama begins.

Yokohama is a harbor city that still retains a maritime flair. It has the biggest Chinatown in Japan, spectacular harborside malls, one of Japan's most famous gardens and is home to one of the major Pokemon Centers.

To get to Yokohama from Tokyo is very simple. The JR Railways has four lines linking Yokohama with Tokyo's main stations. From

Shinjuku and Shibuya, take the JR Shonan-Shinjuku Line (30 minutes from Shinjuku, ¥540). From Tokyo and Shinagawa, take the JR Tokaiso Main Line (25

minutes from Tokyo, ¥470), or the slower, less convenient Yokosuka Line (30 mins, ¥470) and Keihin Tohoku Line Rapid (36 mins).

Sankei-en Garden

 JR Keihin Tohoku Line: Negishi Station (38 mins walk OR + bus ride to get much closer)

 〒231-0824　神奈川県横浜市中区本牧三之谷58-1
58-1, Honmoku Sannotani, Naka-ku, Yokohama, 231-0824

09:00-17:00 (last entry 16:30) Closed for New Years.

¥ 500 yen

 sankeien.or.jp

Sankei-en Garden is a vast classical Japanese garden open to the public and contains many historic buildings. The 175,000 square meter garden was once the private residence of a wealthy silk merchant and has been open to the public since 1906.

It is famed for its plants which reflect the changing seasons.

To reach Sankei-en you will need to take a bus. From Negishi station take bus no. 58, 99 or 101 from bus stop 1. Its a 10-minute ride costing ¥220 yen. Get off at Honmoku, where you have a

10-minute walk to Sankei-en.

Alternatively, from Yokohama Station, take bus 8 or 148 from bus stop 2. It's a 35-minute ride costing ¥220. Get off at Honmoku Sankeien Mae, a 5-minute walk to Sankei-en.

Yokohama Chinatown

 JR: Ishikawacho Station (7 mins)
Minato Mirai Line: Motomachi-Chukagai Station (8 mins)

 ¥ Free

 横浜市中区山下町１３６
136 Yamashitachō, Naka-ku, Yokohama-shi

🕐 Varies from shop to shop, generally 10:00-21:00.

🌐 chinatown.or.jp

Yokohama's Chinatown is a lively collection of Chinese restaurants and shops, centered around the Kanteibyo temple, built in 1873 by the area's Chinese residents and dedicated to the Chinese god of prosperity.

Each entrance to Chinatown is marked by a colorfully decorated gate, with many other architectural flourishes throughout the district.

During Chinese New Year, the area is especially lively, with festivals and events.

Chinatown's main attraction is the food. With restaurants, food stalls, specialty tea shops and Chinese groceries, there's something for every taste.

Yokohama Pokemon Center

 JR: Sakuragicho Station
Minatomirai Line: Minatomirai Station

 ¥ Free

 〒220-0012 神奈川県横浜市西区みなとみらい2-2-1 ランドマークプラザ4F
Landmark Plaza 4F, 2-2-1 Minato Mirai Nishi ku, Yokohama, 220-8172

 10:30 to 20:00

 🌐 pokemon.or.jp

There are Pokemon Centers around Japan, but Yokohama's Pokemon Center, located in the Landmark Plaza, Japan's tallest structured building, is among the biggest.

There are frequent Pikachu parades. The store includes a large variety of Pokemon goods, including some unique to Japan and to the Yokohama store, as well as the chance to battle other Pokemon enthusiasts.

There are smaller Pokemon Centers in Tokyo Station, Narita Airport, Tokyo Skytree, and the Mega-Center in Tokyo's Ikebukuro, as well as part of the Nintendo Store in Shibuya Parko (see page 52).

Yokohama Cup Noodle Museum

 JR: Sakuragicho Station
Minatomirai Line: Minatomirai Station

 ¥ 500 yen

 横市中区新港2-3-4 231-0001
2-3-4 Shinko, Naka-Ku, Yokohama, 231-0001

 Typical opening hours: 10:00-18:00 (Last entry 17:00).
Closed Tuesdays.

 🌐 cupnoodles-museum.jp/english

The Yokohama Cup Noodle Museum explores the history of instant noodles.

It traces the life of its creator, Momofuku Ando, and his discovery through a range of exhibits and

recreations, emphasizing that great discoveries can be made by anyone and on the most humble equipment (Ando came up with the process of preserving noodles in a shed at the back of his

garden).

Other exhibits look at other means of preserving food and offer museum-goers the chance to create their own, individual cup ramen.

Kamakura

Kamakura was the capital of Japan during the Kamakura shogunate, 1185-1333. The town has many temples that date from this period, but it is most famous for the Great Buddha.

Kamakura's sights are spread out throughout the town. In summer, Kamakura's Enoshima Beach is popular with Tokyo residents trying to stay cool. After Tokyo, Kamakura has a relaxing, laid-back feel, and there is an undercurrent of surfing culture.

From Tokyo Station, the quickest and most direct route to Kamakura is via the JR Yokosuka line which takes one hour and costs ¥940.

Once in Kamakura, you'll find an excellent Tourist Information Center at Kamakura station. There are plenty of ways to get around. There is a convenient bus network, Kamakura's Enoden tram system, or you can rent a cycle and explore on your own.

Kotokuin (Great Buddha)

 Enoden Railway: Hase Station (10 mins)

 300 yen (go inside the Great Buddha for 20 yen extra)

 鎌倉市長谷４丁目２番28号
Hase 4-2-28, Kamakura-shi

 April-September: 8:00-17:30 (last entry 17:15), October-March: 8:00-17:00 (last entry 16:45)

 kotoku-in.jp

The Great Buddha is housed at Kotokuin Temple - if housed is the right word. After its last shelter was washed away in a tsunami in 1498, the statue has remained in the open.

The Great Buddha (known as Dai-butsu) is 13.35m high, and weighs 121 tonnes. It was the subject of a poem by Rudyard Kipling, who visited it in 1892.

The statue is hollow on the inside and you can step inside for a better view of the statue's construction for only ¥20.

Hakone

Hakone is an area of high-volcanic activity resulting in ideal *onsen* conditions conveniently close to Tokyo. You can walk portions of the trail through cedar forests, and peek at the sulphuric springs caused by the active volcano at Owakudani. There are numerous galleries, indoor and out, taking advantage of Hakone's scenic beauty as well as many hiking opportunities.

The fastest way to get to Hakone from Tokyo is to take the Kodama Tokaido Shinkansen to Odawara and transfer to the Odakyu Hakone-Tozan line. The trip takes about one hour and costs ¥3,930. While the Shinkansen is covered by the JR Rail Pass, the Odakyu is a private company. Rail Pass holders will have to pay ¥320 for the Odakyu portion of the journey.

To save money, take the regular Tokaido Line to Odawara for ¥1490, and transfer to the Osakyu Hakone-Tozan line at Odawara (¥1,660 total - 2-hour journey). Another alternative is taking the Odakyu Odawara line from Shinjuku, plus Hakone-Tozan line to Hakone (2 hours - ¥1,220).

Once in Hakone, the Hakone-Tozan line, bus networks and pirate ships (no, really) connect Hakone's myriad of attractions. It is easy to get around.

Grab a brochure from the tourist information center near Hakone-Yumoto Station and you are good to go. The Hakone Freepass gives you a return trip on the Odakyu-trains (including the train to/from Shinjuku), unlimited travel on Hakone's trains, buses, pirate ships and cable car, and discounts are tourist hotspots. Follow the 'Hakone Loop' to make the most of the pass. From Shinjuku, a 2-day ticket is ¥5,700, a 3-day ticket is ¥6,100. Purchase from Odakyu stations.

Owakudani

 Hakone-Tozan Line: Souzan Station

 足柄下郡箱根強羅
Hakone, Gora, Ashigarashimo

 Fares from ¥800 to ¥1,480 one-way; ¥1,430 to ¥2,600 roundtrip depending on distance.

 09:00-17:00

 kanagawa-park.or.jp/owakudani & hakoneropeway.co.jp

From Souzan Station, ride the Hakone ropeway up to the Owakudani Ropeway Station.

You can get a good view of the crater by taking the connecting ropeway to Ubako and Gotendai station, on the shore of Lake Ashinoko. The eerie, smoke-filled valley is an ominous reminder of the power of the volcano beneath.

You will appreciate your next hot-spring bath in an entirely new way.

Due to the volatility of the volcano, parts of the ropeway may be shut at short notice. When parts of the ropeway are closed, buses transport passengers between the stations.

Hakone Sekisho (Check Point)

 Bus stop: Onshi Koen Mae

 ¥ 500 yen

〒250-0521 神奈川県足柄下郡箱根町箱根1番地
Hakone 1, Hakone-machi, Ashigarashimo-gun Postcode: 250-0521

09:00-17:00 (last entry 16:30), Winter: December-February:
09:00-16:30 (last entry 16:00)

hakonesekisyo.jp

Hakone Checkpoint was the largest and most important of the 53 checkpoints the Tokugawa shogunate established on the roads to Edo.

Built in 1619, the checkpoint was designed to police guns going into Edo and women coming out. As the wives and families of the feudal lords were held in Edo as hostages to secure good behavior and loyalty to the shogun, the Hakone checkpoint surveyed women very closely.

Models and other exhibits demonstrate the form the inspection took.

A live performance (in Japanese), between two unfortunate travelers and a checkpoint official, takes place periodically, further illustrating its use.

In the cedar forest surrounding the Hakone Checkpoint, portions of the Tokaido Trail still exist and make for a pleasant hike, even in summer, when the shade of the trees prevents you from becoming too hot.

To reach the Hakone checkpoint, take the Hakone-Tozan bus to Onshi Koen Mae (¥980, 40 minutes).

Fuji Fivi Lakes

The Fuji Five Lakes district is located to the North of Mount Fuji. The area includes the mountain itself, the lakes, a large amount of forest for hiking, as well as caves formed by the movement of lava, museums, galleries, onsen, the Fuji-Q theme park and other tourist attractions. It is becoming increasingly popular for outdoor activities, including hiking, kayaking, and cycling.

From Shinjuku, you can board buses to Fuji-Q Highland (1 hour 40 mins/ ¥2,000), Kawaguchi-ko Station (1 hour 45 mins/ ¥2,000), or the fifth station on Mt. Fuji itself (2 hours 30 mins/¥2,950 May-October only). Tickets can be reserved online at highway-buses.jp.

From Tokyo Station, you can take the trains. Ride the JR Chuo line to Otsuki (1 hour 49 minutes/¥1,520), and transfer to the Fujikyu Railway to Kawaguchiko station (1 hour/¥1,170). Look out for fast trains that do the journey in less time. The bus makes more sense in reality.

Once in the Fuji Five Lakes area, there is an extensive local bus network with Kawaguchiko Station as its hub. The Tourist Information Center is beside Kawaguchiko Station, and can help you figure out what bus to get to your destination as well as providing information about the Five Lakes' myriad of attractions. Another option is to rent a cycle. Many of the cycle rental companies will store your luggage while you ride.

Mt. Fuji

 Fujikyu Railway/
Highway Buses:
Kawaguchiko Station
/ JR Minobu Line:
Fujinomiya Station

 Free

 Tourist Information:
山梨県南都留郡 富
士河口湖町船津３
６４１‒１ (3641-1
Funatsu Fujikawag-
uchikomachi,
Minamitsuru-gun,
Yamanashi)

 fujisan-climb.jp

 Early-July to mid-
September

Mt. Fuji is Japan's tallest mountain at 3776 meters. It's also a potentially active volcano and a sacred site.

Many Japanese people climb Fuji as a pilgrimage, not simply a physical challenge. The mountain is traditionally approached via the Murayama Sengen Jinja, a shrine at Mt. Fuji's base, but most climbers start at the Fuji 5th station.

Seeing the sunrise from the top of Mt. Fuji is the goal of many climbers, and most start the six-hour climb late at night in order to reach the summit for the sunrise. Another option is to climb during the day and spent the night on the mountain in one of the huts (reservation necessary).

There are four different climbing routes up Mt Fuji. Each is divided into ten stations, with public transport going as far as the fifth. The routes are: the Fuji-Subaru trail (most popular, ascent 5-7 hours, descent 3-5 hours, very accessible, huts at the 7th and 8th stations), Subashiri trail (ascent 5-8 hours, descent 3-5 hours, connects with the Yoshida trail at the 8th station), Gotemba trail (ascent 7-10 hours, descent 3-6 hours, four huts at the 8th station), and the Fujinomiya trail (ascent 4-7 hours, descent 2-4 hours, six huts along the trail).

Mt. Fuji is not considered a particularly difficult or challenging hike, but every year climbers are caught off guard by weather or get into other difficulties (eg. altitude sickness from descending too fast).

For inexperienced or anxious climbers, guided tours are offered by travel agencies within Japan.

The official climbing season is July to mid-September only (exact dates vary year to year). Even at this time, the height of the Japanese summer, temperatures on top of Fuji can drop below freezing.

Don't be misled by the sight of old Japanese men making the climb. It is important to respect Fuji and prepare seriously, especially if you decide to attempt Fuji off-season.

Outside of the climbing season, buses stop running to the fifth station, and the only options are a long walk or a taxi (about ¥13,000 one way).

If climbing in the off-season, you should lodge a climbing plan by filling out a form at a local police station before you start.

Fuji-Q Highland

 Fujikyu Highway Bus (from Shinjuku, Tokyo, Shibuya, Yokohama and Haneda Airport)/Keio Highway Bus (from Shinjuku): Fuji-Q Highland.

 〒403-0017 山梨県富士吉田市新西原5-6-1
5-6-1 Shin-Nishihara. Fujiyoshida, Yamanashi Prefecture 403-0017 Japan

 Opening hours 9:30, closing hours vary by season and peak and off-peak days. In winter, the earliest closing time is 17:00.

 1 day 'Free Pass': ¥6,000. Combo with train tickets also sold.

fujiq.jp

Fuji Q-Highland is the biggest of Japan's homegrown theme parks, and provides a large number of extreme rides, including four world-record-holding coasters, the world's longest haunted house, and much more!

There are child-friendly rides as well, including Thomas World, a Thomas the Tank Engine area within the theme park.

Views of Mt. Fuji are on offer from various points around the park, and there are several restaurants on-site as well.

Saiko Bat Cave

 Bus stop: Komori-Ana Iriguchi

 南都留郡富士河口湖町西湖２６０８
2068 Saiko, Fujikawaguchiko-machi, Minami-tsuru-gun

 09:00-17:00 March 20th to November 20th

 800 yen

 fujisan.ne.jp

Saiko Bat Cave is the largest of the natural lava caves around Mt. Fuji.

The 350m length cave has a very steady temperature throughout the year, and has become the nesting area for three different kinds of bat.

You can enter the cave and follow the clearly marked out trail. To protect the bats from visitors, the part of the cave where the bats sleep during the day is closed off, but you can still catch a glimpse of them. The cafe is a depository for all sorts of Batman items.

Nikko

Nikko is a small town, but its two major temples are some of the most beautiful and important in all of Japan.

It's here, among the mountains, still forested and peaceful, that Tokugawa Ieyasu wished to be enshrined as a god. His descendants acted on his wishes, with Nikko becoming the location of the Tokugawa shogunate's mausoleums. The mausoleums are quite unlike other Japanese

temples, with gaudy decorations and Chinese influence.

There are two temples founded in the eighth century by Shodo Shonin, the monk who introduced Buddhism to Nikko, and the famous Shinkyo bridge, historically used only by the shogun.

Nikko's atmosphere of peace is well worth the two-hour train ride to get here, provided that you time your trip to avoid the hordes of

students who visit on school trips.

Nikko is served by JR and Tobu Lines. The JR Lines are more expensive unless you have a Japan Rail Pass. From Tokyo Station, take the Tsubasa or Yamabiko Shinkansen to Utsunomiya station, and transfer to the local Nikko line. The journey takes 112 minutes and costs ¥5,480.

The Tobu Lines originate at the Tobu Asakusa Station in

Asakusa. From there hourly trains go directly to Nikko. The trip takes 142 minutes, costing ¥1,360.

A number of passes are aimed at foreign tourists spending a few days exploring Nikko and its surroundings (there is hiking and a hot spring frequented by monkeys), are available from the Tobu Sightseeing Center at Asakusa Station. For ¥4,600, the Nikko All Area Pass offers unlimited transport on certain buses and trains in Nikko and Kinugawa for 4 days (this includes a return trip between Nikko and Tokyo on the Tobu Line).

From Nikko Station, you can either walk the 2 km to the Toshogu shrines or catch a bus. The Tobu bus from stop 2C outside Tobu Nikko Station takes 6 minutes to the shrines and costs ¥260.

Nikko Toshogu Temple and Shrine

 Bus-stop: Hotel-Seikoen-Mae   1300 yen

 日光市山内２３０１
2301 Sannai, Nikko-shi

 April-October: 9:00-17:00, November-March: 9:00-16:00 toshogu.jp

Toshogu is unique in many ways. Dating from 1636, the temple structures feel old in a way that Tokyo's temples just don't.

Toshogu was constructed around the natural scenery of Nikko's mountain forest and has a transcendent, calming atmosphere. Toshogu consists of a temple and various temple buildings including multiple gates, pagodas, prayer houses and an outer and inner temple (where Tokugawa Ieyasu is buried).

The carvings are particularly noteworthy, serving both as religious instruction and decoration. Make sure you don't miss the three wise monkeys or the sleeping cat. Carved by master craftsman Hidari Jingorou, the cat is said to be so realistic that it frightens mice away from Toshogu's buildings. The elephants are interesting for different reasons, clearly carved by someone with no idea what an elephant looked like. Toshogu also has a stable with a horse donated by the New Zealand government.

Taiyuinbyo

 Bus-Stop: Taiyuin Futarasan-jinja mae   400-550 yen for 1 shrine, 900 yen for all

 日光市山内2300
2300 Sannai Nikko-shi

 April-October: 8:00-17:00 (last entry 16:30), November-March: 8:00-16:00 (last entry 15:30) rinnoji.or.jp

Smaller than Toshogu, Taiyuinbyo was built to enshrine Ieyasu's grandson Iemitsu, the third shogun, who was responsible for rebuilding Toshogu in its present form.

As it is smaller, it is less busy, and has a more peaceful atmosphere, allowing you time to properly appreciate the beauty of the buildings.

Of particular note are the richly decorated Nitenmon gate, white dragon sculpture and the mausoleum itself. You can only view the mausoleum and main temple building from the outside.

Shopping

Tokyo has everything, from big-name international brands, flagship stores and mega-malls to forgotten neighborhoods plying everyday goods and flea markets. Rather than offering a definitive guide, this section gives a few examples of the various kinds of shopping establishments around.

Most of the major stations are surrounded by shopping buildings, with Shinjuku and Ikebukuro stations being built into malls.

Department stores offer upmarket goods at top prices, including foreign brands like Louis Vuitton and Hermes.

For casual street fashion, Shibuya and its many shopping neighborhoods is the place to go.

Finally, if you are a fan of Japanese cooking and want some authentic souvenirs to take home with you, you can't miss the outer market at Tsukiji, with its large collection of fresh ingredients at wholesale prices, or Ameyoko and Kappabashi shopping streets. There is nowhere better than a flea market or antique fair for a unique find.

Japanese goods, while expensive at first glance, tend to be extremely high quality. The clothing chain Uniqlo is definitely worth checking out, particularly in winter for its heat-tech clothing line. In summer, their Airism range of underclothes keeps you cool.

Mitsukoshi Department Store

 Tokyo Metro: Ginza Station   10:00-20:00

There are a few Mitsukoshi Department Stores in Tokyo, but while all of them offer a selection of luxury goods at top prices, the Ginza department store is the original and has the best foreign language support.

There is English speaking staff at the service counter and a foreign tourist information office in the basement with money exchange services. There is even tax-free shopping available.

Mitsukoshi preserves the by-gone era of the department store with opulent surroundings, gloved staff bowing to waiting customers before they open the door every morning and impeccable service.

It is the place to go for handbags, watches and shoes, though unfortunately the latter do not come in larger sizes.

Mitsukoshi also has a good selection of Japanese fashion, interior design goods and traditional crafts sourced from all over Japan.

The basement floor has an amazing range of fresh produce and exquisitely decorated cakes and sweets, ranging from the traditional sweets served in the tea ceremony to European style cakes and pastries. There are usually samples on offer.

The restaurant floors have a selection of Japanese, Asian and Western restaurants and there are tea and coffee shops throughout the store.

Yodobashi Camera Shinjuku

 JR: Shinjuku Station

 9:30-22:00

Yodobashi Camera is a chain of electronics stores. The Shinjuku branch is the main store and comprises of thirteen surrounding shops and buildings.

At its center is the 9-floor Multimedia Pavilion, instantly recognizable to anyone who has been to Shinjuku at night.

Inside, the store is plastered with advertisements in every spare space, while the store's theme music plays on repeat. It is a sensory overload, but if you can make it into the store, you'll find every kind of electronic good imaginable on display. If you're after a camera, however, you'll want to go across the road to the dedicated Camera Pavilion. If making a purchase, check that the manual comes in English.

Solamachi

 Tobu Skytree Line: Tokyo Skytree Station
Tokyo Metro and Narita Sky Access Keisei Line: Oshiage Station (5 mins).

 10:00-21:00 (6F 7F 30F 31F restaurants open 11:00-23:00)

Solamachi is a shopping complex at the base of the Tokyo Skytree. It is the modern answer to the department store, with four restaurant floors, and countless entertainment options, including an aquarium and a planetarium, and all manner of shops.

Solamachi contains Japanese chain stores such as Uniqlo (high-quality clothing at affordable prices), Loft (cute stationery and quirky lifestyle goods), as well as a Pokemon Center, Hello Kitty and Disney Store.

Solamachi has many facilities for foreign tourists. 70 of Solamachi's 300 stores offer duty-free shopping, and the Sumida Industry and Tourism Information Center is located on the first floor. Many of the restaurants offer English menus and vegetarian options. The Solamachi website has suggestions for unique Japanese souvenirs. See the Sumida neighborhood guide for additional information about Solamachi.

Roppongi Hills

 Tokyo Metro: Roppongi Station   Shops: 11:00-21:00. Restaurants: 11:00-23:00

Roppongi Hills is a mega-complex located in Tokyo's Roppongi district.

At 27 acres, it is one of Japan's largest integrated developments and was ground-breaking when it opened in 2003. It includes apartments, office space, shops, restaurants, cafés, movie theaters, a hotel, museum, galleries and parks, and is centered around the Mori Building, location of the Tokyo City View Observation Deck and Mori Art Museum.

Designer Mori Minoru's vision was for a self-sufficient city within a city, eliminating the need for people to commute, thus improving their quality of life by allowing more leisure

hours. The Mori Tower has many big-name occupants, including Apple Japan's offices and the Pokemon Company headquarters.

Shops within Roppongi Hills

primarily focus on accessories, fashion and interior design. There are a large number of restaurants, offering Japanese and European food.

Yoyogi Flea Market

 JR: Harajuku Station
Tokyo Metro: Meiji Jingu Mae 'Harajuku' Station

 10:00-16:00

Resale and vintage fashions are slow to take root in Japan, where the trend tends towards disposing of consumer goods.

There are a few second-hand shops in Harajuku's back alleys, and the big Book-Off, Off-House and Hard-Off stores have used electronics, brand goods, music instruments, games, books and clothing.

For sheer fun and atmosphere, however, you cannot pass up Yoyogi Flea Market.

Held in Yoyogi Park, walking distance from Harajuku's main shopping street, the Yoyogi Flea Market is committed to recycling. No professional sellers are allowed. Sellers and shoppers tend to be younger. You can often snap up cutting edge Japanese

fashion items at heavily reduced prices. The market takes place on a Sunday 10:00-16:00. The dates vary, so check the park's schedule at yoyogipark.info (Flea market is written フリーマーケット).

Yoyogi Park also hosts the Earth Day Market (アースデイマーケット) once a month, selling organic produce, fair trade goods and tasty street food.

Oedo Antique Market

 JR and Tokyo Metro: Yurakucho Station

9:00-16:00, 1st & 3rd Sat of the month.

Tokyo's Oedo Antique Market is the largest outdoor market in Japan. It takes place in the grounds of the Tokyo International Forum, the modern design of the building's architecture an interesting counterpoint to the goods on sale.

The name 'Oedo' is a reference to the Edo period, intended to evoke the workmanship and

craftsmanship of the period rather than provide a timeframe for the goods on sale.

The market specializes in Japanese craft items. Two-thirds of the vendors sell Japanese antiques. To find out what the other third offer, you'll have to visit!

Palette Town

 Rinkai Line: Tokyo Teleport Station

Shops: 11:00-21:00. Restaurants: 11:00-23:00.

Odaiba's Palette Town is another mega-complex that contains amusement spots, shops, restaurants and one of the world's largest Ferris wheels.

Other Palette Town attractions include Venus Fort, a fashion shopping mall modeled on Venetian architecture, the teamLab Borderless art gallery, and Toyota Motors 'Mega web' showroom.

Palette Town also contains Leisure Land, open twenty-four hours and offering a variety of amusements, including karaoke, bowling, arcade games and a haunted house.

Venus Fort is primarily aimed at women, with most stores offering women's clothing, accessories and shoes in a variety of styles and prices, but there are also plenty of places to eat.

There are also stores selling luggage and interior design objects. Attached to Venus Fort is Sun Walk, a complex with shops for pet-owners.

Shibuya Shopping District

 JR and Tokyo Metro: Shibuya Station   Typically 10:00-21:00

Youth fashion moved to Shibuya in the 1970s and never left. The big-name brand stores occupy the shopping malls and buildings in the blocks surrounding Shibuya Station and the famous pedestrian crossing.

Independent stores with quirkier fashions can be found in the smaller side streets and in Shibuya's neighborhoods, many of which have a unique fashion flavor.

Harajuku is firmly associated with the gothic lolita styles that blend elements of goth fashion with Victorian and Rococo stylistic flourishes. However, it is a pop culture center and many American brands have stores in Harajuku, including Forever 21.

The Harajuku Laforet building houses a selection of fashion stores, including a large children's toy store. The closest station is JR Harajuku Station.

Omotesando and Cat Street are pleasant boulevards lined by up-market fashion or unique one-of-a-kind boutiques. Both are easily accessible from Tokyo Metro Omotesando Station. See the Shibuya neighborhood guide for additional information.

Tsukiji Outer Market

 Tokyo Metro Hibiya Line: Tsukiji Station (5 mins)
Tokyo Metro Oedo Line: Tsukiji-Shijo Station (7 mins)

 Mostly 09:00-14:00. Closed Sundays.

Tsukiji Fish Market's (the old home of the tuna auctions) outer market offers an excellent selection of Japanese cooking ingredients, utensils and clothing at wholesale prices.

Since the market is primarily aimed at Japanese restaurant owners, the majority of goods will not be of interest to the casual tourist.

However, there is a selection of items that make excellent and authentic souvenirs and gifts. Tea, Japanese pottery, cooking knives, dried seaweed and other preserved food items, and Japanese clothing are among the items on offer at Tsukiji's outer market.

Unlike Western-style markets and those in many other Asian countries, bargaining is frowned upon and sellers as a rule do not deviate from the prices displayed on their stalls.

Ameyoko

 JR Lines: Ueno Station or Okachimachi Station Keisei Line or Tokyo Metro: Ueno Station

 Generally 10:00-20:00, closed Wed

There is no longer a black market operating in Ueno's Ameyoko, but the street market is still the place to go for a bargain on fresh fish, vegetables, fruits and Japanese style cooking implements.

If you're shopping for unique Japanese snacks, its worth paying the market a visit.

There is a theory that the 'ame' in ameyoko is a reference to candy and there are still several stalls serving up sweets, including a stall specializing in discount chocolate.

If you don't find anything in Ameyoko, try the side streets around Ueno. These are home to funky and fun fashion, accessories and lifestyle goods that Tokyo is famous for.

Kappabashi Shopping Street

 Tokyo Metro: Tawaramachi Station

Generally 09:00-17:00. Closed Sundays and national holidays.

Kappabashi Shopping Street is the place to go for anything restaurant and cooking related, whether it is cooking pots, utensils, plastic food for your shop display, paper lanterns or neon 'open' signs. The shopping street is about 800 meters long, and packed with tiny shops jam-packed with goods.

For most foreign tourists, the atmosphere of Kappabashi is more of an attraction than the shopping itself, but there are still some good souvenir finds. Chopsticks make great gifts, while a plastic model of your favorite Tokyo meal makes a good gag gift, or a unique keepsake.

Performances, Music & Arts

Tokyo doesn't have a counterpart to London's West End or New York's Broadway, but there are plenty of entertainment options - in Japanese. English language productions are limited to tours by international casts from Broadway shows and are relatively rare. Still, for the Broadway fan, Shiki Theatre's Japanese language adaptions of Broadway shows are bound to be interesting, while the spectacle and glitz of Takarazuka Theatre's all-female shows entertain, even if you have no idea what is being said on stage.

Performances

Kabuki-za
Website: kabuki-za.co.jp

Kabuki-za hosts grand performances of *Kabuki* daily. *Kabuki* is a traditional form of theatre that developed amongst the merchant and craftsmen classes of Edo's downtown as a counterpart to the stylized *Noh* drama enjoyed by the aristocrats.

Kabuki is characterized by garish masks, exaggerated gestures and language so old that even Japanese people struggle to understand it.

Kabuki-za is extremely foreigner-friendly and has English headsets with an audio guide available to rent.

You can buy tickets for a single act or a whole show. Seats usually range in cost from ¥3,000-8,000.

AKB48
Address: AKB48 Theater 〒 101-0021 東京都千代田区 外神田４丁目３-３ (Sotokanda 4-3-3, Chiyoda-ku, Tokyo Postcode: 101-0021)
Website: www.akb48.co.jp/theater/

AKB48 is a pop idol group named for Akihabara (AKB) and the number of members (now expanded to 130, ranging from young teens to women in their mid-twenties). AKB48 was formed around the concept of a group that performed live daily so that fans could always see and interact with them. AKB48 members are arranged in teams that rotate.

The group is a pop phenomenon, releasing several best-selling singles. Although there are live performances at the AKB48 theater daily, tickets are assigned by lottery, so you can apply in advance but you can't be sure you will get to see a performance until the day before when you get a confirmation e-mail if successful.

Music and Arts

Bunkamura
Nearest Station: JR and Tokyo Metro: Shibuya Station (7 mins)
Address: 〒150-8507　東京都渋谷区道玄坂2-24-1 (2-24-1 Dogenzaka, Shibuya-ku Postcode: 150-8507)
Phone: 03-3477-9111
Website: bunkamura.co.jp

Bunkamura is a concert hall, theater, cinema, shopping complex and museum located in Shibuya. Its Orchard Hall is the home of the Tokyo Philharmonic Orchestra, the oldest classical orchestra in Japan. It is also a venue for the Tokyo International Film Festival. A free shuttle bus runs between Shibuya station's Miyamasuzaka Exit and the Bunkamura between 9:50-20:15.

New National Theatre Tokyo
Nearest Station: Keio Line: Hatsudai Station
Address: 〒151-0071　東京都渋谷区本町1丁目1番1号 (1-1-1, Hon-machi, Shibuya-ku, Tokyo 151-0071 JAPAN)
Phone: 03-5351-3011
Website: nntt.jac.go.jp/english/

The New National Theatre Tokyo hosts performances of opera, ballet, dance and drama by Japanese casts.

Suntory Hall
Nearest Station: Tokyo Metro: Tameike-Sanno Station
Address: 東京都港区赤坂1-13-1 (Akasaka 1-13-1, Minato-ku, Tokyo Postcode: 107-8403)
Phone:03-3505-1001
Website: suntory.com/

culture-sports/suntoryhall/

Suntory Hall is a concert hall consisting of two halls, the Main Hall and the Small Hall. It was described as "a jewel box of sound" by Herbert von Karajan, Austrian composer and conductor of the Berlin Philharmonic orchestra, who is commemorated by a statue outside the hall.

Tokyu Theatre Orb
Nearest Station: JR and Tokyo Metro: Shibuya Station
Address: 東京都渋谷区渋谷2-21-1 渋谷ヒカリエ11階 (Shibuya Hikarie 11F 2-21-1 Shibuya, Shibuya-ku, Tokyo)
Phone: 03-347705858
Website: theatre-orb.com

Describing itself as 'the theatre in mid-air', Theatre Orb hosts musicals, both visiting International casts and Japanese cast adaptations. For performances in English, Japanese subtitles are shown.

Nissay Theatre
Nearest Station: Tokyo Metro and Toei Subway: Hibiya Station

Address: 東京都千代田区有楽町1-1-1 (1-1-1 Yurakucho, Chiyoda-ku, Tokyo, Japan Postcode: 100-0006)
Phone: 03-3503-3111
Website: nissaytheatre.or.jp

Located in Chiyoda, the Nissay Theatre was built in 1963. Throughout its long career, the theatre has hosted opera, *kabuki* and musicals. It was the home-theatre of the Shiki Theatre Group until they moved to their own theatre.

Takarazuka Theater
Nearest Station: Tokyo Metro and Toei Subway: Hibiya Station
Address: 東京都千代田区有楽町1-1-3 (1-1-3 Yurakucho, Chiyoda-ku, Tokyo, Japan Postcode: 100-0006)
Phone: 03-5251-2001
Website: kageki.hankyu.co.jp/english/theater/tokyo.html

The Takarazuka Theatre troupe is an all-woman theatre troupe originating in Osaka. Early in their training, the actors specialize in female or male roles, and hone their feminine and masculine gestures and actions.

Takazuka shows tend to be glamorous, lavish affairs, either adaptations of already existing international shows or original productions.

They are known for the Takarazaka revue, where they perform a medley of show tunes, with over-the-top costumes worthy of Vegas. The actors have a cult following among their fans, with fan groups assembling outside the theater every morning to wish the actors a good day's work and again at night to congratulate them on their performance.

Performances are entirely in Japanese. There is a store in the theatre that sells Takarazuka goods.

Theatre Creation
Nearest Station: Tokyo Metro and Toei Subway : Hibiya Station
Address: 東京都千代田区有楽町1-2-1 (1-2-1 Yurakucho, Chiyoda-ku, Tokyo)
Phone: 03-3201-7777
Website:toho.co.jp/stage/theatre_crea/

Theatre Creation's previous line-up has included a pop-rock adaptation of Shakespeare's As You Like It, the Japanese cast version of Rent, the musical adaptation of Legally Blonde and a cluster of other Japanese shows.

The Shiki Theatre Company
Nearest Station: JR Lines: Hamamatsucho Station
Address: 〒105-0022 東京都港区海岸1-10-48 (1-10-48 Kaigan, Minato-ku, TOKYO 105-0022)
Phone: 03-5776-6730
Website: www.shiki.jp

Japan's best known and largest theatre company, the Shiki Theatre Company has 8 home theatres across Japan including 3 in Tokyo, all found in Minato.

The Shiki Theatre HARU is the biggest, hosting premiere performances of West End and Broadway musicals. The Shiki Theatre stage original productions, but are best known for their Japanese language productions of Broadway Musicals.

Musical fans will enjoy the chance to see how the familiar stories and songs are adapted to Japanese culture.

An interesting difference to note is that rather than giving a cast a standing ovation, Japanese audiences indicate their satisfaction with a performance by continuing to clap for a long time.

Akasaka ACT Theater
Nearest Station: Tokyo Metro: Akasaka Station
Address: 東京都港区赤坂 5-3-2 赤坂サカス内 (Akasaka Sakasunai Akasaka 5-3-2, Minato-ku, Tokyo)
Phone: 03-3589-2277
Website: tbs.co.jp/act/

The Akasaka ACT Theater is a commercial theatre in Akasaka owned by TBS. The theatre has hosted some major productions, including The Phantom of the Opera and Billy Elliott. It hosts a mix of musicals and Japanese productions.

Nightlife

Tokyo has many nightlife options, from izakaya, the traditional pubs, to show pubs that offer a burlesque-style performance with your meal. Roppongi is considered the best clubbing district, while Shibuya has an active LGBTQIA+ scene. In the alleys of Shinjuku's Kabukicho district are host and hostess clubs and snack bars. The legal drinking age in Japan is 20.

Bars and Pubs

Bar Trench (Shibuya)
Nearest Station: JR and Tokyo Metro: Ebisu Station (5 mins)
Address: 渋谷区恵比寿西1-5-8DISビル102 (1-5-8 Ebisunishi Shibuya Tokyo)
Phone: 03-3780-5291
Website: small-axe.net/bar-trench/

Bar Trench is furnished in French *fin de siècle* style and offers an incredible range of spirits, including herbal liqueurs and absinthe. The menu offers foods that you might not expect to find in Tokyo. Bar Trench is small but worth a visit.

Bar Candy (Shinjuku)
Nearest Station: JR & Tokyo Metro: Shinjuku Station
Address: 〒160-0022新宿3-35-12B1F バー キャンテ イー 新宿 (3-35-12 Shinjuku | B1F, Shinjuku 160-0022)
Phone: 03-3354-3720
Website:facebook.com/BarCANDYShinjuku

A cocktail bar hidden among Shinjuku's winding streets. Entry is free for foreigners. Drinks are cheap and the friendly bartender/owner goes out of his way to make guests feel welcome.

New York Bar (Shinjuku)
Nearest Station: Tokyo Metro and JR: Nishi Shinjuku Station (16 mins)

Address: パーク ハイアット 東京 東京都新宿区西新宿3-7-1-2 (3-7-1-2 Nishi Shinjuku, Tokyo, 52nd floor)
Phone: 03-5323-3458
Website: tokyo.park.hyatt.com

Lost in Translation was filmed almost entirely in Shinjuku and Shibuya and many of the film locations are actual bars and restaurants. Bob spends most of his nights at the New York Bar, atop the Park Hyatt Tokyo—and you can, too!

The bar is open to non-hotel guests, but it isn't cheap. A bottle of Japanese beer starts at ¥1,000 and there is a ¥2,000 cover charge after 20:00 (19:00 on Sundays). A dress code applies.

Sanchoku-ya
Nearest Station: Keio Inokashira Line: Shinsen Station
Address: 渋谷区円山町12-2 ライオンズマンション渋谷　B1F 東京都渋谷区, 東京都 (Basement floor, 12-2, Maruyama-cho, Shibuya-ku, Tokyo)
Website: Reservations taken at facebook.com/santyokuya.taka

Sanchoku-ya is a Japanese style *izakaya* that serves traditional style fish dishes

alongside a variety of *sake* (Japanese rice wine). Sanchoku-ya takes the guesswork out of ordering by offering course menus only, which you select when you make your reservation (one-week in advance reservations are necessary—Sanchoku is popular).

Sanchoku serves seafood dishes with unlimited sake refills. The menu is entirely up to the chef and changes regularly to take advantage of seasonal delicacies.

Yorozuya Okagesan
Nearest Station: JR and Tokyo Metro: Yotsuya Station
Address: 東京都新宿区四谷2－10 松本館（たんす専門店 地下1階）(Matsumoto-kan B1, Yotsuya 2-10, Shinjuku-ku, Tokyo)
Phone: 03-3355-8100

Website: okagesan.net

Yorozuya Okagesan is a traditional style *izakaya* in the mold of most of Shinjuku's traditional pubs— a small basement restaurant with a friendly atmosphere.

The restaurant has a Michelin one-star rating, and it is impossible to get a table without a reservation.

The chef used to be a rock star. He now presides over a kitchen and an impressive sake cellar. The menu is extensive, but it is best to order the *'omakase* set'— basically, the chef's recommendation—for seasonal dishes at the height of freshness. Okagesan's highlight is the mixed sashimi platter.

Izakaya Vin
Nearest Station: JR & Tokyo Metro: Shibuya Station
Address: 東京都渋谷区道玄坂1丁目 5-7 (1-5-7 Dogenzaka, Shibuya-ku, Tokyo)
Phone: 03-3496-2467

Despite the *'izakaya'* in its name, Izakaya Vin has a sophisticated French vibe.

Its staff are enthusiastic and knowledgeable about the wine and champagne they serve, available by the glass or the bottle.

The food is *bistro* style and comes in plentiful portions, unusual in *izakaya*, but heavy on the meat with few vegetarian options.

Show Pubs

Show pubs are a modern Japanese phenomenon, combining elements of *geisha* tradition but updating them for a new generation. Shows vary in tone, but these are not strip shows and a suitable standard of behavior is expected from guests.

Roppongi Kaguwa
Nearest Station: Tokyo Metro and Toei Subway: Roppongi Station (5 mins)
Address: 東京都港区六本木5-4-2 六本木香和 (Roppongi KAGUWA 5-4-2 Roppongi Minato-ku Tokyo)
Phone: 03-5414-8818
Website: kaguwa-roppongi.com

The show at Roppongi Kaguwa takes its inspiration from *Oiran* (courtesans),

samurai and *geisha*, with a stage show that combines contemporary and traditional elements of Japanese culture.

The emphasis is on the performance, with a skilled cast that pulls of aerial manoeuvres and intense dance sequences. Suggestive rather than provocative.

Dinner is a fusion of Japanese and Western dishes and comes with free drinks, including a selection of soft drinks. Vegetarian options are available.

Burlesque Tokyo
Nearest Station: Tokyo Metro and Toei Subway: Roppongi Station
Address: 〒106 - 0032 東京

都港区六本木7 - 13 - 2 アーバンビル7F (Urban-biru 7F Roppongi 7-13-2, Minato-ku, Tokyo)
Phone: 03-6447-2037
Website: burlesque-roppongi.com

Inspired by the film Burlesque, Burlesque Tokyo puts on a musical cabaret show with a provocative edge.

The vibe is definitely seedier and more modern than its competitors, with an atmosphere that has been described as 'bachelor-stag-party.'

The loud music and smokey atmosphere make this feel more like a club than a show pub.

Clubs

Sound Museum Vision (Shibuya)

Nearest Station: JR and Tokyo Metro: Shibuya Station (10 mins)
Address: 〒150-0043道玄坂 2-10-7-B1F サウンドミュージアムビジョン (B1F 2-10-7 Dogenzaka, Shibuya)
Phone: 03-5728-2824
Website: vision-tokyo.com

Reliably strong music and DJ performances that always draws a good-sized crowd. The Gaia and Deep Space room are for dancing, while the White and D-lounge provide a place to chat. Admission is ¥3,500.

AgeHa

Nearest Station: JR and Tokyo Metro: Shinkiba Station (5 mins). Free Shuttle buses run between Shibuya and AgeHa from 23:30 to 05:00.
Address: 〒136-0082新木場 2-2-10 (2-2-10 Shinkiba, Koto 136-0082, Tokyo)
Phone: 03-5534-2525
Website: ageha.com

A true crowd-pleaser, hosting a ton of events throughout the year, including frequent gay nights. The Halloween party is not to be missed. There are nights when women can enter for free (though they still need to buy a drink ticket). Admission varies depending on events, but expect to pay ¥3500.

Womb

Nearest Station: JR and Tokyo Metro: Shibuya Station (10 mins)
Address: 〒150-0044円山町 2-16 ウーム (2-16 Maruyama-cho, Shibuya 150-0044, Tokyo)
Phone: 03 5459-0039
Website: womb.co.jp

Womb is an atmospheric club with a laser show and a dance floor that is standing room only during big events. The DJs vary considerably in skill, so if you're picky about music, it is best to check the line-up in advance and consider going to nearby Sound Museum Vision instead.

LGBTQIA+

Most of Tokyo's LGBTQIA+ scene centers around Shinjuku-ni-chome (新宿2 丁目) where you'll find a variety of bars, some with dance floors, some without.

Campy Bar

Nearest Station: JR Lines/ Tokyo Metro/Toei Subway: Shinjuku Station
Address: 東京都新宿区歌 舞伎町2-13-10 (2-13-10 Shinjuku, Shinjuku-ku Tokyo)
Website: campy.jp

Run by a celebrity cross-dresser, Campy Bar is staffed by drag queens. It has a fun, welcoming atmosphere and is open to everyone. It doesn't have a cover charge (unless you reserve a sofa at the weekend). Worth a visit for the vibe alone.

Suzu Bar

Nearest Station: JR/Tokyo Metro/Toei Subway: Shinjuku Station
Address: 東京都新宿区歌 舞伎町1−1−1 01F (1-1-10 Kabukicho, Shinjuku-ku Tokyo)
Phone: 03-5272-6100
Website: facebook.com/ suzubar.shinjuku

Suzu rocks a 1950's craft aesthetic which gives this mid-sized bar a unique ambiance.

It is run by LGBT activist Fumino Sugiyama and has an extensive cocktail menu.

Sport

Japan's national sport is sumo, but its most popular sport is baseball, with soccer, thanks to the success of the women's team, Nadeshiko Japan, gaining rapidly in popularity. There are opportunities to see all of these sports - and more - in Tokyo.

Tokyo Dome

 JR/Tokyo Metro/Toei Subway: Suidobashi Station

 東京都文京区超楽後楽1-3-61
(1 Chome-3-61 Koraku, Bunkyo, Tokyo 112-0004)

 tokyo-dome.co.jp

Nicknamed 'The Big Egg,' Tokyo Dome is a 55,000-capacity stadium, built in 1988. The dome's roof is an unusual air-supported structure, sustained by slightly pressurizing the air inside the stadium.

The Tokyo Dome is the home stadium of the Yomiuri Giants baseball team, the oldest team still playing in the Japanese professional Leagues.

They're also one of the strongest Japanese baseball teams, and have an ongoing rivalry with Osaka's Hanshin tigers.

In addition to baseball games, the Tokyo Dome hosts concerts, basketball, pro-wrestling, American football, mixed martial arts, kick-boxing and monster truck events.

It is part of Tokyo Dome City, a surrounding shopping and entertainment complex that houses the Japanese Baseball Hall of Fame.

Ajinomoto Stadium

 Keio Line: Tobitakyu Station (5 mins)   東京都調布市西町376-3
376-3, Nishimachi, Chofu-shi, Tokyo   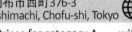 ajinomotostadium.com

Ajinomoto Stadium is a multi-purpose stadium located in Chofu, Tokyo.

It is the home stadium of two football (soccer) clubs, the J League Division One team F.C. Tokyo, and Division Two team Tokyo Verdy. Ajinomoto Stadium also hosts Rugby Union and American Football games.

Tickets can be purchased online or from convenience stores. Prices for category A, the most popular games, range from ¥2500-6000. Category B games range from ¥2,000-5000.

Tours of the stadium, lasting one hour, are available on dates listed on the official website. Reservations are essential.

The stadium will be a venue during the 2020/2021 Tokyo Olympics, but in keeping with the Olympic committee rules about advertising (Ajinomoto is a commercial sponsor), the stadium will be called Tokyo Stadium.

Ajinomoto Stadium often hosts non-sports related events such as concerts and flea-markets. Following the 2011 Tohoku Earthquake and resulting Tsunami, the stadium was used as a shelter for survivors.

Meiji Jingu Stadium (Shinjuku)

 Tokyo Metro: Gaienmae Station (5 mins)
Toei Subway: Kokuritsu-Kyogijo Station (12 mins)

 東京都新宿区霞ケ丘町3-1 (3-1, Kasumigaokacho, Shinjuku, Tokyo)

 jingu-stadium.com

In operation since 1926, Meiji Jingu Stadium is a baseball stadium in Shinjuku, and home to the professional baseball team, the Yakult Swallows. It also hosts University games.

The stadium is owned by Meiji Jingu shrine. Among its many claims to fame is that it is one of the few surviving stadiums that Babe Ruth played at.

It also hosted an exhibition match as part of the 1964 Tokyo Olympic Games. For more, see the Shinjuku neighborhood guide.

Ryogoku Kokugikan (Sumida)

 JR and Toei Subway: Ryogoku Station

 東京都墨田区横綱1丁目3-28 1-3-28 Yokoduna, Sumida-ku, Tokyo

 sumo.pia.jp

In January, May and September, Ryogoku Kokugikan hosts 3 of the 6 official sumo tournaments. If you're in Tokyo at that time, it's worth attempting to get a chair at one of them.

Chairs come in a range of prices suitable for any budget, and tournaments are all-day affairs, so you can wander in and out.

Outside of the tournaments, the Ryogoku Kokugikan has a small museum. It's worth checking out the neighboring sumo stables for the chance to see the wrestlers at their morning practice, or maybe even spot a few as they head to the neighboring restaurants for *chanko-nabe*, a hot pot dish designed to help sumo wrestlers bulk up.

For more, see the Sumida neighborhood guide.

Nissan Stadium (Yokohama)

 JR: Shin-Yokohama Station

 〒222-0036 横浜市港北区小机町3300 (3300 Kozukue-cho,Kohoku-ku, Yokohama City 222-0036)

 nissan-stadium.jp

Nissan Stadium Yokohama, also known as International Stadium Yokohama, has the highest seating capacity of any stadium in Japan, with 72,327 seats. It is the home stadium of the Yokohama F. Marinos, a soccer team that competes in the J-League Division One.

The stadium hosted games during the 2002 FIFA world cup, and the final game in the 2019 Rugby World Cup.

The stadium hosts English tours of about an hour long. Book through the official website. It is known as the International Stadium Yokohama for the 2020 Olympics.

Japan National Stadium

The former National Stadium was demolished and, on its site, the new National Stadium was constructed. It is a multi-purpose stadium that will serve as the main venue for the postponed 2020 Tokyo Olympics in summer 2021. The Japan Olympic Museum is also nearby (¥500 admission fee).

Dining

Tokyo has some of the world's best dining, ranging from exquisitely prepared Kaiseki (traditional Japanese course menu of fresh seasonal ingredients), to cheap ramen, bowls of Chinese-style noodles, consumed in hole in the wall restaurants in the seedy alleys of Kabukicho.

In our experience, it is hard to find bad food in Tokyo. The Japanese have high standards when it comes to food, and even the most disreputable-looking bars and restaurants will have high standards of hygiene. Enjoy the ambiance. It's all part of the fun of dining in Tokyo.

No guide to Tokyo's dining scene could ever be complete, as new restaurants open on a daily basis. Instead, this section offers a brief guide to various kinds of Japanese food with some suggestions of where to try them.

For a special night out, consult the Luxury Dining section for an introduction to some of Tokyo's Michelin star restaurants.

Finally, affordable dining covers cheaper restaurants that don't fall into either of the above categories.

For more up to date recommendations, grab a copy of Hot Pepper, a free magazine that chronicles Tokyo's restaurant scene (magazine.hotpepper.jp).

Although the magazine is in Japanese, the pictures make it easy to get an idea of what is on offer at each restaurant. The only hard part is choosing which one to visit.

Japanese Cuisine
Kaiseki

Kaiseki, or *kaiseki-ryori* to give its full Japanese definition, is the Japanese equivalent of haute-cuisine. It is a multi-course dinner of high-quality seasonal ingredients, served in small portions, with emphasis laid on the freshness, subtle flavoring intended to bring out the natural flavors of the food, and presentation of each dish.

Modern *kaiseki* draws from pre-existing traditions, notably *shonin-ryori*, food prepared according to Buddhist principles, and the tea ceremony.

Most *kaiseki* meals will include an appetizer, sashimi, a steamed dish, grilled dish, some form of soup, a bowl of rice and a sweet. Japanese tend to order *kaiseki* meals when entertaining business clients, or to accompany *enkai*, drinking parties, most notably the *bon-nen-kai* at the end of the year.

Morikawa Akasaka (東京都港区赤坂3-21-6/Akasaka 3-21-6 Minato-ku Tokyo) is considered the best *kaiseki* restaurant in Tokyo. Unfortunately, it does not take reservations from first-time guests. You need an invitation from a current client. Dinner starts at ¥30,000.

Akasaka Eigetsu (東京都港区赤坂３−１１−７ソシアル赤坂ビル4F/Social Akasaka Building 4F, 3-11-7 Akasaka Minato-ku Tokyo) has only ten seats making reservations essential. Three kinds of courses are available at ¥12,000, ¥15,000 and ¥20,000 per person.

Tokyo Shiba Tofu-ya Ukai (東京都港区芝公園4-4-13/4-4-13 Shiba-koen, Minato-ku, Tokyo)—see Minato neighborhood guide.

Izakaya

Often described as Japanese pubs, *izakaya* come in a range of styles, from smoky dens where customers sit on *tatami* to bistros with a decidedly European vibe.

Customers don't go to an *izakaya* for a quick meal, they go to spend several hours. There will be a wide range of drinks available.

As soon as customers are seated, it is usual to be served an appetizer, which will be charged in lieu of a cover charge.

Izakaya serve small dishes intended to be shared among a group of guests. *Izakaya* typically have a good selection of Japanese spirits, including local beers, sake and *sho-chu*, usually distilled from sweet potato, barley or rice. *Ume-shu* is a sweet plum liqueur, good for casual drinkers.

Aomori Izakaya Garugaru (歌舞伎町1-6-6橋本ビル2階/ 1-6-6 Kabukicho | 2F Hashimoto Bldg., Shinjuku) is a fairly typical Japanese style *Izakaya*. Appetizers start from ¥600.

Sushi Izakaya Macchan (東京都港区六本木7-13-11/7-13-11 Roppongi, Minato) as an inexpensive *izakaya* in Roppongi, popular with the locals. It's a good place for delicious sushi that won't break the bank.

Izakaya Suzunoya (東京都台東区浅草2-7-13/2-7-13 Asakusa, Taito) - A large part of the *izakaya* experience is the interaction with the owner. At Suzunoya, the friendly owner goes out of his way to welcome guests.

Shokudo

Shokudo is cafeteria-style dining. There are two types available. Self-service where you fill a tray with your desired items, or Set-Meals, where you order a main dish, accompanied by sides, generally miso-soup, a bowl of rice, and a cup of tea.

Shokudo are cheap, intended to provide quick, filling meals for Tokyo's workforce. They are a good

way to try Japanese home-style cooking without the price tag of an *izakaya*.

D47 Shokudo (東京都渋谷区丁目21-1渋谷ヒカリエ8 F/ 8F Shibuya Hikarie Bldg., Shibuya 21-1) is located within walking distance of Shibuya station. The menu changes frequently, incorporating regional specialties from around Japan. Closed

Wednesdays.

Nagi Shokudo (東京都渋谷区鶯谷町15-10/15-10 Uguisudanicho, Shibuya) offers a good number of vegan dishes heavily inspired by traditional *shojin-ryori* (Buddhist cuisine).

The menu is frequently updated to take advantage of seasonal produce.

Grilled

There are two main styles of grilled meat served in Japan. *Yakitori* are skewers, usually of chicken although the menu has expanded to include vegetables, served in tiny, smoky bars. The most authentic way to try *yakitori* is a hole-in-the-wall bar in Yurakucho or Kabukicho.

Yakiniku are barbeque restaurants, often Korean inspired, where you order slices of beef, chicken, pork,

seafood and vegetables, which you then cook to your liking over a grill at your table. Both types of restaurants are a lot of fun, but be warned that you will come away smelling of smoke.

Yakitori no Hachibei (東京都港区六本木6-10-1 六本木ヒルズウエストウォーク5F/ 5F Roppongi Hills West Walk 6-10-1 Roppongi, Minato, Tokyo) is a *yakitori*

restaurant with a wide menu, including a few unusual options—horse sashimi, anyone?

Yakiniku Jumbo Shirogane (東京都港区白金3-1-1/ 3-1-1 Shirogane, Minato) serves premium meats from all over Japan and a selection of Korean sides, including *kimchi* and *bibimbap*. The beef is especially good.

Sashimi & Sushi

Sashimi is fine slices of fresh raw fish. Sushi is thin slices of raw or lightly seared fish served on vinegar-rice, or in a roll with toasted seaweed.

Sashimi is generally served as part of a course meal in *kaiseki-ryori*, or ordered as an individual item from an *izakaya*. The cheapest way to enjoy sashimi is by buying a tray from a supermarket.

There are many dedicated sushi restaurants in Tokyo, from up-market restaurants that serve sushi courses to conveyer belt restaurants that offer a selection of sushi

cheaply. The best place to eat sushi in Tokyo is the area surrounding the former Tsukiji Fish Market or at the new Toyosu Fish Market, but almost every neighbourhood has its own sushi place.

Sushi Yoshitake (東京都中央区銀座 8-7-19 すずりゅうビル 3 F /3 Suzuryu Building 8-7-19 Ginza, Chuo-ku) is a Michelin 3-star sushi restaurant that seats seven. Chef Masahiro Yoshitake is unafraid to depart from the traditional and create new and flavorsome sushi combinations.

Kaikaya (東京都渋谷区円山町 23-7/ 23-7 Maruyamacho, Shibuya, Tokyo) is a more typical sushi restaurant. The staff is welcoming and happy to explain unfamiliar dishes in English.

Uobei Shibuya Dogenzaka (東京都渋谷区道玄坂2-29-11第六セントラルビル 1F/Dai-roku Central Bldg. 1F, 2-29-11 Dogenzaka, Shibuya) is a conveyor-belt sushi restaurant. You can order off the menu through the touch-screen mounted above the counter or take plates of sushi directly from the belt.

Noodles

There are three main varieties of noodles served in Japan. *Udon* are thick wheat noodles that soak up the broth they are served in. *Soba* are buckwheat noodles served in hot soup in winter, and chilled in summer. *Ramen* are Chinese-style noodles served in a soup-like brother.

You will see countless shops offering noodle dishes everywhere you go in Tokyo, from department store restaurant floors to tiny hole-

in-the-wall places, and street stalls. Although cheap, noodles make a delicious, filling meal.

Ramen Nagi (東京都新宿区歌舞伎町1-1-102F/2F 1-1-10 Kabukicho, Shinjuku) is a tiny ramen restaurant squeezed into Kabukicho. It is a testament to Nagi's ramen that even in Kabukicho, which has the most bars per square foot in the world, people wait to eat here.

Udon Shin (東京都渋谷区代々木2-20-16相馬ビル1F/1F Soma Bldg 2-20-16 Yoyogi Shibuya) is an udon restaurant that rates extremely highly with Tokyo locals.

Soba Dining Daian (東京都新宿3-36-6大安ビル2階/ 2F Daian Bldg, 3-36-6 Shinjuku) boasts hand-made soba noodles made as you watch by the chef. It is pricier than usual for soba restaurants, offering an up-market take on this classic.

Fried

Japan has a number of unique dishes prepared on either a hotplate or by frying.

Okonomiyaki, with a base of thinly sliced cabbage, cooked in a batter, is a staple throughout Japan. In Tokyo, the local variation is *monjayaki*. *Teppanyaki* is thinly sliced meat or vegetables cooked in front of you by a chef. *Tonkatsu* is a breaded pork cutlet, crispy on the outside, succulent within, served with a variety of sides.

Tempura often accompanies noodle dishes, or is a separate course as part of a *kaiseki* menu.

Sakura Tei (東京都渋谷区神宮前3-20-1/ 3-20-1 Jingumae, Shibuya) offers both *okonomiyaki* and *monjayaki*. The friendly staff will help you cook your meal if you need assistance.

Teppanyaki Akasaka (東京都港区赤坂1-12-33ANAインターコンチネンタルホテル

東京37F/ANA InterContinental Tokyo 37F 1-12-33 Akasaka) is a great date location, with excellent views, a personal chef for the evening and exquisite food.

Marugo Tonkatsu (千代田区外神田1-8-14/ 1-8-14 Sotokanda, Chiyoda) is located in Akihabara and considered one of the best *tonkatsu* restaurants in Tokyo. Try the pork and shrimp set that comes with rice, miso soup and salad.

Hot Pot

Nabe or 'pot' is synonymous with a style of cooking where diners cook a selection of ingredients in a common pot at their table.

This style of cooking includes *sukiyaki*, as well as *chanko-nabe*, a protein-heavy hot-pot dish consumed by sumo wrestlers. For the best *chanko-nabe* head to Ryogoku (see the Sumida neighborhood guide).

Hyotan Nabe Kaminarimon (東京都台東区浅草1-2-9/ 1-2-9 Asakusa, Taito) offers *nabe* as well as *okonomiyaki*, *monjayaki* and do it yourself teppanyaki dishes. Fantastic atmosphere with friendly staff, who make up for lack of English ability by being extremely helpful and friendly.

Chanko Nabe Ryokoku Shinjuku Gyoen-Mae (東京都新宿区新宿1-34-13貝塚ビル1F/1F Kaizuka Biru 1-34-13 Shinjuku, Shinjuku-ku)

is owned by a former professional sumo wrestler and prides itself on its authentic *chanko-nabe*. Walking distance from Shinjuku.

Luxury Dining

Tokyo is the world's best food city according to the Michelin guide, which has awarded over 300 stars to restaurants in Tokyo, the most ever given out to any one city. This list is merely a selection.

Omotesando Ukai-tei (東京都渋谷区神宮前5-10-1表参道ジャイル5F / 5F Omotesando Gyre, 5-10-1 Jingu-mae, Shibuya-ku, Tokyo 150-0001) is a *teppanyaki* restaurant located in a 150-year-old building off the Omotesando cooking street. Food has a distinct French influence. Lunch courses start at ¥6,600, dinner courses from ¥19,800. Desserts are served in a separate European-style tearoom.

Mikawa Zezankyo (江東区福住 1-3-1 / 1-3-1 Fukuju, Koto-ku) is a Michelin one-star *tempura* restaurant where every piece of *tempura* is personally fried by Chef Tetsuya Saotome, often described as a living treasure. The restaurant has only nine seats, making for an intimate

dining experience. Saotome follows the Edomae tradition, using only ingredients available during the Edo-period. The Omakase Course is priced at ¥20,900 including tax.

Kikunoi (東京都港区赤坂6-13-8 /6-13-8 Akasaka, Minato-ku) is one of the best *kaiseki* restaurants in Tokyo. Chef Yoshihiro Murata has three restaurants with a total of seven Michelin stars between them. He is a Japanese cooking super-star and even has his own TV show. Chef Murata's book explaining the nuances of *kaiseki* cuisine in English, and an English menu ensure that you eat with confidence. Lunch offers the choice between a lunch box at ¥5000, or a course meal for ¥10,000. Dinner starts at ¥16,000.

Quintessence (品川区北品川6-7-29 ガーデンシティ品川　御殿山 1 F/Shinagawa-Ku Kitashinagawa 6-7-29 Garden City Shinagawa Gotenyama 1F) is a

contemporary French restaurant where the menu changes daily. Quintessence prides itself on *cuisson*, a technique of roasting meat for a long time at a low temperature to bring out the most flavor from the meat. Dinner is ¥26,500. The extensive wine cellar has 600 varieties of wine on offer.

Kanda (東京都港区元麻布三－六－三四 カーム元麻布一階/ Calm Motoazabu, 3-6-34 Motoazabu, Minato-ku, Tokyo) puts a modern twist on Japanese cuisine. The restaurant has 3 Michelin stars. Rather than off-putting, the minimalist decor creates a cozy ambiance with diners often finding themselves in conversation with the chef. All the staff speaks excellent English.

Kanda prides itself on impeccable service and the quality and intensity of its

dishes. The degustation sets are ¥20,000, ¥25,000 and ¥30,000.

Affordable Dining
Fusion dishes

Japan has many variations on international dishes, which, while not exactly authentic, are delicious and often available more cheaply than dining at a specialty restaurant.

You don't need to go out of your way to find them either. All the dishes in this section can be found on the menu of most restaurants (with the exception of *kaiseki*).

Omu-raisu (omelet-rice) is fried rice, usually flavored with tomato sauce, onion and occasionally chicken, wrapped in a delicate omelet. It is popular with children. Grill Grand (東京都

台東区浅草3-24-6 / 3-24-6 Asakusa, Taito-ku) has been serving omuraisu since 1941, and is famous for its demi-glace sauce.

Hamburg steaks are seasoned hamburger patties served without the bun. Sakana No Nakasei (東京都中央区日本橋室町2-3-1 コレド室町2 B1F / Tokyo-to, Chuo-ku, Nihonbashi 2-3-1 Coredo Muromachi 2, Basement Level 1) is best left to the seasoned hamburg fan as it allows you to customize everything from how the mince is ground to what ingredients are added to the patty before cooking.

Kuroke (croquette), also known as **menchi**, is a small meat or potato patty, breaded and deep-fried to crunchy perfection. Asakusa Menchi (東京都台東区浅草2-3-3 / 2-3-3 Asakusa Taito, Tokyo) offers only one kind of *menchi*, made from beef and pork, with sweet onion and spices.

Kare (curry), also **kare-raisu** (curry-rice) bears no relation to Indian curry. It's more like a savory stew than curry. Regardless, it is extremely popular. CoCo Ichibanya is a chain restaurant that specializes in Japanese curry. You can find it throughout Tokyo.

Japanese Fast Food chains

Yoshinoya, Sukiya, Tenya and Ootoya - These fast food chains specialize in Japanese-style cooking adapted to the fast pace of modern life. You will be surprised at the quality of the food and the size of the portions. These restaurants are a way to eat relatively healthily for cheap while in Tokyo.

Mos Burger, Freshness Burger, Lotteria, First Kitchen and Beckers - These are Japanese versions of

hamburger restaurants. While MOS Burger and Freshness Burger tend to be slightly better for you than their American counterparts, none of these are exactly healthy choices, though cheap and delicious.

Soup Stock Tokyo - The best fast-food option for anyone wanting to get their recommended serving of vegetables or with dietary needs (vegetarian soups are available and it's possible to

eat gluten-free here). Soup stock has soups made with fresh, seasonal vegetables, available on their own or as part of a set menu with rice or bread and a drink.

Saizeriya - Good, cheap Italian food, Saizeriya offers incredibly good food for some of the lowest prices around. Saizeriya's menu includes lunch specials and a variety of vegetable sides.

Family Restaurants

Family restaurants tend to be open 24 hours, making them great places to hang out while waiting for late-night buses or if you arrived on an early flight. Typically Family restaurants offer a salad bar or a drink bar, which means that you can help yourself to as much salad or soft drinks (including tea and coffee) as you want. Prominent Family Restaurant chains throughout Tokyo include Jonathan's, Denny's and Royal Host.

Tokyo on a Budget

Tokyo is one of the most expensive cities in the world to live, but a visit doesn't need to break the bank. The key is being organized, doing your research ahead of time and knowing exactly what you want to prioritize when working out your budget. Tokyo has a number of budget-friendly options available to the frugal traveler.

❶ Save on Flights and Accommodation

The biggest cost of visiting Tokyo is getting there. A number of budget airlines fly to Tokyo including Jetstar, Spring Airlines and China Eastern Airlines. Use sites like Google Flights, Expedia.com, SkyScanner.net and Kayak.com to compare flights. Try adjusting your travel dates and traveling mid-week where possible. Sign up to airlines' newsletters to get advance notifications of their sales.

The cheapest accommodation in Tokyo is hostels. There are a number of hostel chains with branches across Tokyo, especially in Asakusa including Khaosan, Sakura Hotel and Hostel, J-Hoppers, and YHA Japan. Hostels in Japan are clean, safe and comfortable. The biggest downside is the noise. A pair of earplugs and a sleeping mask can make a huge difference here. If staying for a long time, some hostels offer reduced or free board in exchange for cleaning. These opportunities are advertised on noticeboards in the reception.

Astep up from hostels are budget business hotels. Chains include the Toyoko Inn and APA. It is worth joining their membership program simply for the discount offered on rooms.

AirBNB is slowly taking root in Tokyo, although adoption is low. For long stays, consider a share-house, offering a private room with a shared kitchen, laundry and bathroom. Sakura Hotel and Hostel operates a share-house in Tokyo.

Hotels in Japan tend to charge peak and off-peak rates, with prices going up during periods of high demand such as weekends, national holidays, the cherry-blossom season Check the National Holidays section for an idea of dates to avoid.

❷ Getting Around

Once in Tokyo, stick to public transport as much as possible. Use sites like hyperdia.com/en to compare different train routes. By traveling on rapids and locals, and avoiding trains with a seat reservation charge, you can reduce your costs.

When you're navigating Tokyo, plan your days to visit attractions that are near each other as much as possible. It is worth spending some time on Google Maps working out where the attractions you're most interested in are in relation to each other. The results may surprise you. Although the Nezu Museum is in Minato, it is closer to Shibuya than other Minato attractions, for example.

There are several discount passes available for use on Tokyo's train and subway services, but these are not always a good deal. Do the math ahead of time to make sure you'll use the pass. If you can limit yourself to traveling by subway only, you'll save a lot. Buying a prepaid Suica or Pasmo card gives you a slight discount on all fares, and can be used across Tokyo. Refer to the Transport in Tokyo chapter.

❸ Food

Conbini, convenience stores are everywhere in Tokyo. Look for Lawson, FamilyMart, 7-11 and the like. They offer freshly baked bread, *onigiri*, salads, fruit, snacks and drinks for prices comparable with supermarkets. You can buy two *onigiri* and a coffee from a *conbini* for roughly ¥450, a huge saving compared to the ¥1000-2000 charged by hotels for breakfast.

If your hostel or share-house has a kitchen, doing your own cooking can save you money. Most hostels have common-use seasonings. Daiso, the ¥100 store, has a surprising selection of quick cook meals and ingredients. Head to supermarkets in residential neighborhoods to get your groceries. Fresh fruit in particular can be very expensive.

Tokyo has a wide range of affordable restaurants, and even those with the strictest budget should be able to dine out once a day. When eating out, grab a copy of Hot Pepper. This free magazine often includes coupons to the restaurants it features. Also, when selecting a restaurant, particularly an *izakaya* or bar, ask about the cover charge before you sit down to avoid an unpleasant surprise when the bill arrives.

❹ Daiso

Daiso in a chain of ¥100 stores. They are everywhere in Tokyo. Compared to dollar stores in the US and other countries, Daiso goods are of surprisingly high quality. If you need to buy anything during your trip to Japan, including sleeping pillows, luggage tags, neckties, stationery, earplugs, socks, it is always worth going by a Daiso first. Chances are they'll have what you need for a lot less than you would pay anywhere else.

Among the goods that Daiso has on offer are erasers in the shape of Japanese food items, cute and colorful notepaper and envelopes, cooking utensils, chopsticks, snacks and Japanese pottery, any of which make great presents for friends and family back home.

Seasonal Events

Tokyo always has something interesting and different going on whenever you visit. Here is a month by month list of some of the events throughout the year.

January

New Years Day - January 1 to 3

Crowds start gathering late December 31st at Tokyo's major shrines, ready to pay the ceremonial first shrine visit of the New Year.

Meiji Jingu Shrine in particular draws huge crowds, and a festive atmosphere. If large numbers of people don't make you claustrophobic, join them to see in the New Year in true Japanese fashion. The shrine continues to draw large crowds several days after New Years Day.

Because January 1 is a national holiday and many Japanese leave Tokyo to travel home, many businesses, restaurants and tourist attractions close over the New Years—including ATMs. If staying in Japan over this time, it is worth checking that your hostel or ryokan (if small) will stay open, and making sure you have enough cash to keep you over the holiday period.

If you find yourself stuck, some *conbini* (convenience store) ATMs work even throughout the New Year period.

Coming of Age Day - Second Monday in January

Coming of Age Day celebrates those who have reached the age of majority, 20 years old. Coming of Age ceremonies are held at prefectural and local government offices, followed by after-parties held by families.

Women usually adopt elaborate formal *kimono* (usually rented) and elaborate hairstyles to commemorate the occasion. It is common for the *kimono* to be paired with a white fur muff, the only time these are combined.

A few men wear *hakama*, the corresponding formal kimono for men, but most opt for a Western-style suit.

February

Chinese New Year - Late Jan and Early Feb

Yokohama's Chinatown puts on a massive show during the Chinese New Year's festival with parades, seasonal foods, and other events.

There is never a bad time to head to Chinatown, but Chinese New Year is definitely one of the best!

Festivities include traditional lion dances and a Lantern festival held around Masobyo Temple.

Setsubun - 2 Feb 2021

Setsubun is a purification ceremony, where evil spirits are dispelled by throwing dried beans at them.

Usually, a member of a family will wear a paper 'demon' mask, symbolizing misfortune, and other members of the household will drive him or her out. This festival is especially popular with children who enjoy throwing beans.

Stores sell a variety of bean related goods, including candied red-beans, and *maki-zushi*, sushi rolls, which are believed to have lucky connotations if eaten on Setsubun.

Shinto-shrines and Buddhist temples celebrate Setsubun with festivals, with priests and invited guests, throwing roasted soybeans, candy, and envelopes of money to the eager crowd.

Festivities at Senso-ji in Asakusa are the biggest in the country, attracting crowds of around 10,000 people. The *Fukuju-no-Mai* dance, one of the temple's three famous rituals, is performed.

At Nishi-Arai, the Daruma Kuyo festival takes place. Daruma are small figurines brought for luck. People return previously purchased *daruma* to the shrine and

purchase new ones.

The old *daruma* are burned in a solemn purification ritual led by priests in full ceremonial garb. Gojo Tenjinja in Ueno park also hosts an elaborate Setsubun ritual known as Ukera Shinto Ritual.

Plum Blossom Festivals - Mid Feb to Early March

Yushima Tenmangu Shrine has been renowned for its plum blossoms since the Edo period. When the plum blossoms are in full bloom, a festival takes place at the shrine.

If you will miss the cherry blossom, don't miss this chance to experience

Japanese blossom fever.

Setagaya Ume Festival celebrates the plum blossom with koto performances, tea ceremonies, rice cake pounding and other festivities held at the weekends while the trees are in flower.

Edo Nagashibina - Late Feb to Early March

Nagashibina is a protection ritual where disasters that can befall children are imbued in dolls made of paper and sent down the river to draw disaster away from real children. About 1,500 people are allowed to participate in this event and are chosen by lot.

March

Tokyo Marathon - 7 March 2021

The Tokyo Marathon is one of six World Marathon Majors, an IAAF certified gold-level marathon, that takes place annually in Tokyo.

There are far more applicants than there are places.

The day before the Tokyo Marathon, the Tokyo Marathon Family Run, for parents and children, and the Tokyo Marathon Friendship Run, for Japanese runners to interact with International runners, takes place.

Takao-san Fire Walking Festival - Mid-March

A fire-walking festival takes place annually at Mt. Takao's Yakuoin Temple.

Festival goers pray for the safety of their loved ones, then follow in the footsteps of the monks over the still smoldering ashes of the sacred fire.

By the time the general public gets to it, the fire is well and truly out and there is no danger.

If you want to participate, bring a towel to clean your feet afterward.

Asakusa Kannon Kigen-e - 18 March

March 18 is the day that the two fishermen brothers fished a beautiful statue of Kannon out of the Sumida river, leading to the founding of Senso-ji temple.

To celebrate the founding of the temple, the *Kinryu no Mai* (Golden dragon) dance is performed at Senso-ji every year on this date

Cherry Blossom Season - Late March to Early April

As soon as the cherry blossom starts to bloom, Tokyo rushes to admire the fragile blossoms. Multiple cherry blossom viewing festivals spring up in Tokyo's famous sakura-viewing locations. Notable cherry blossom celebrations take place at:

- Nihonbashi Sakura Festival

- Naka-Meguro Sakura Festival (see Meguro River, Shibuya)
- Chiyodoriguchi Sakura Festival (see Chidoriguchi, Chiyoda)

Ueno Sakura Festival
- Weeping Cherry Tree Light Up Event, Rikugien Gardens
- Sumida Park Sakura Festival

April

Asakusa Senso-ji Temple Events

Three big events take place at Senso-ji temple throughout April.

Hana Matsuri: (April 8) - A flower festival to celebrate Buddha's birthday. School children form a procession pulling a white elephant, and temple visitors are served hydrangea tea.

Ichiyo Sakura Matsuri - Festivities include stage shows and markets. The highlight is the Edo Yoshiwara Oiran-dochu Parade, replicating a procession that took place during the Edo period. The Parade takes place on the second Saturday of April.

Shirasagi-no-Mai (White Heron Dance) takes place mid-April and is the revival of a Heian period tradition. A parade takes place with dancers wearing Heian-period costumes.

Yabusame (Horseback Archery) - Mid-April

Yabusame is a horseback archery display. Originally part of the New Year's festivities during the Edo-period, the tradition continues at Sumida Park.

Elaborately costumed riders take turns to attempt to hit targets that line the course.

After the display, the arrows and slivers of the targets that were hit are sold as good luck charms.

The *yabusame* is followed by *kusajishi*, shooting at targets made of grass, and a parade.

Kameido Tenjin Shrine Wisteria Festival - Late Apr to Early May

The wisteria that blooms in the grounds of Kameido Tenjin Shrine was planted in the Edo period. The fifth and eighth Tokugawa shoguns are among those who have visited to admire the blossoms, and the wisteria blooms have been depicted in *ukiyo-e* woodcuts.

May

Kanda Festival - Early May to Mid May

The Kanda festival is one of the three great festivals of Edo. It is six days of celebration, though most crowds gather the two days of processions.

The *Shinko-sai* parade sees a procession of *mikoshi*, portable shrines, carried from Kanda to Nihombashi, to the Ote-Marunouchi district, before making their way to Akihabara and back to the shrine.

During the *Mikoshi Miya-ri* procession, hundreds of floats prepared by residents are brought to the shrine.

This is a fantastic opportunity to witness (and if you're lucky, participate in) one of the biggest festivals of its kind in Japan.

Due to an ancient feud with Hie shrine's Sanno Festival and clashes between their competing parades, the Kanda Festival and Sanno Festival take it in turns to hold their parades on successive years.

The Kanda festival takes place on odd-numbered years. The next parade will take place 2021, and then 2023.

Sanja Matsuri - Mid-May

Along with the Kanda festival, the Sanja Festival is one of Edo's three famous festivals.

The Sanja Festival is a celebration of Senso-ji's founding. Unlike other festivals that take place at Senso-ji, this is not a Buddhist tradition.

Rather, it is attached to the Shinto shrine commemorating the fishermen brothers and the village headman who are responsible for the temple's founding. Portable *mikoshi* shrines are paraded through the neighboring streets,

June

Torikoe Jinja Annual Festival - Early to Mid-June

Torikoe Shrine is a 1360-year-old shrine that holds its annual festival in June. The festival includes a parade, including people in costume, traditional dances and a *mikoshi*, a portable shrine. Torikoe Shrine's *mikoshi* weighs four tons, and is the heaviest in Tokyo. The event draws thousands of people to Taito, where the festival takes place.

Bunkyo Hydrangea Festival - Early to Mid-June

The city of Bunkyo, where Tokyo Dome is located, is known for its five flower festivals. Early to mid-June, 3000 hydrangea bushes growing at Hakusan Jinja and Hakusan Park come into bloom, bringing a splash of color to the rainy season. Festival stalls are set up throughout the park. Dates vary according to the blooming of the hydrangea.

Tsukiji Shishi Festival - Mid-June

Namiyoke Inari Shrine is a shrine in Tsukiji where people pray for protection from disasters, the safety of those doing construction work and for business prosperity.

The festival gives thanks for the reclamation of the surrounding land in the Edo

period.

The parade consists of huge floats with a lion's head, a dragon's head and a tiger-head symbolizing the deities who control the earth, clouds and wind.

Sanno Festival - Around 15 June

Sanno is one of the three great festivals of Edo centering around Hie Shrine. It's also one of the largest festivals in Japan.

The festival lasts eleven days, with something different happening every day. There is a formal prayer ceremony, and an

abundance of traditional Japanese music and dance, ikebana, tea ceremony and historic costumes. The highlight is the Shinkosai parade, in which Hie shrine's *mikoshi*, portable shrine, is paraded through central Tokyo.

Due to an ancient feud with

Kanda shrine and clashes between their competing parades, the Sanno Festival and Kanda festival take it in turns to hold their parades on successive years. The Sanno Festival takes place on even-numbered years.

The next parade will take place in 2022.

July

Sumida River Fireworks Festival - Late July

Summer is the time for fireworks displays in Tokyo, and the Sumida River display is one of the biggest, oldest and best.

Follow the crowds of young people in *yukata*, light summer *kimono*, to the river between Sakura-bashi bridge and Kototoi-bashi bridge, or Komagata-bashi bridge to Umaya-bashi bridge.

Alternatively, reserve a spot on a dinner boat for an unforgettable view of the fireworks.

Shinjuku Eisa Festival - Late July

The Eisa Festival originated in Okinawa as part of the Obon observations, honoring the spirits of departed family members and praying for good health and prosperity. Shinjuku's Eisa festival has all the elements of the original, with *teodori*, hand dances, performances of traditional instruments, energetic dances and taiko, traditional drum, performances.

Chiyoda-ku Lantern Floating Event - Mid-July

As part of the Obon observations, residents of Chiyoda release 700 lanterns into the waters of the Imperial moat. Go to Chidorigafuchi from 19:00 to see the lanterns floating down the moat, symbolizing those who have departed before us.

August

Omotesando Super Yosakoi - Late August

Yosakoi is a street dance festival that originated in Kochi.

The Tokyo festival draws dance teams from all over Japan.

Yokasoi is characterized by high energy dance and elaborate costumes. It is a must-see.

It takes place along Omotesando boulevard in Shibuya, near Harajuku.

Asakusa Samba Carnival Parade - Late August

Asakusa's Samba Carnival is the largest in Japan, attracting samba teams from all across the country. The parade includes floats, banners and dance, but the highlight is the elaborate costumes.

September

Meguro Sun Festival - Mid to Late September

The Meguro Kumin Matsuri (Sun Festival) is a large festival, the highlight of which is 5000 Pacific Saury fish grilled over charcoal and served to the waiting crowds. It also includes regional specialty booths, festival booths and booths with activities aimed at children.

October

Tokyo Ramen Show - Late October to Mid-November
Eleven days of the best regional ramen served up at Setagaya's Komozawa Olympic Park.

Tokyo International Film Festival - Late October
Held in Roppongi, Tokyo's International Film Festival takes place over one week. It is accredited by the FIAPF, and includes screenings, seminars and awards.

Kiba no Kakunori (log rolling) - Late October
Koto was once home to Tokyo's lumber yards, and the workmen developed considerable skill at building rafts. Kakunori developed as a way to showcase this skill. Every year, a display of logrolling takes place as part of the local festival, keeping the traditions of the area alive.

November

Chrysanthemum Festivals
November is the month for Chrysanthemums, with various temples and gardens around Tokyo putting on displays of this flower.

Some of the most notable can be seen at: Yushima Tenjin Shrine, Kongo-ji Temple, Meiji Jingu, Asakusa Senso-ji Temple and Shinjuku Gyoen.

Kagurazaka Street Oedo Tour (Shinjuku) - Mid-November
The streets of Kagurazaka become a stage for traditional Japanese performing arts. Leading artists demonstrate the various styles of performance that evolved in Kagurazaka.

Shichi-go-san - 15 November
Shichi-go-san, or 7-5-3 is a festival celebrating the rite of passage for Japanese children who have made it to the ages of 3 and 5 for boys, and 3 and 7 for girls. Traditionally, 3 was the age at which children were allowed to grow their hair out, 5 was the age boys were first dressed in *hakama*, the male *kimono*, and 7 the age that girls swapped the simple cord tying their *kimono* for an obi, a decorative waistband. Today, children are dressed in formal wear, either Japanese or Western, and taken to a shrine to give thanks and pray for the child's continued well-being.

Hachioji Ginkgo Festival - Mid-November
Most autumn leaf festivals in Japan revolve around the maple, but when Hachioji's *gingko* trees turn yellow, the town celebrates with a festival that includes orienteering challenges, a parade of classic cars and a celebration of everything Showa, the period when the trees were planted.

December

Illuminations
From mid-November through to January, large parts of Tokyo are lit up after dark with glittering light displays. Some, but not all, are Christmas themed.

Some of the more prominent are:
- Festival of Light, Takenotsuka
- Winter Vista Illumination, Showa Kinen Park
- Caretta Illumination, Shiodome
- Minamilumi, Shinjuku
- Midtown Christmas, Tokyo Midtown (Roppongi)
- Artelligent Christmas, Roppongi Hills
- Jewel Dome, Nakameguro
- Blue Cave, Shibuya
- Christmas Illuminations, Ginza
- Odaiba Illuminations
- Winter Illumination, Tokyo Dome City
- White Circus, Akasaka (features a skating rink)

Itinerary: Tokyo in a Week
Day One - Monday

Enjoy a leisurely visit to the **Imperial Palace East Gardens**. Get a takeaway coffee and a pastry from one of the many bakeries in Tokyo Station's underway mall and walk 10 minutes to the palace grounds for a picnic.

Stroll through the gardens, taking in the Edo-period garden and Niju-bashi bridge. If you're not too jet-lagged, rent a boat and row around the Imperial moat, or, join the many joggers on a counter-clockwise circuit of the Imperial Gardens course.

Return to **Tokyo Station**, taking photos of the historic

Marunouchi facade, before heading to the surrounding skyscrapers for lunch. The seventh floor of the Shin-Marunouchi building and the fifth floor of the Marunouchi building have manycafés and restaurants with good food and views over Tokyo Station.

After lunch, head inside Tokyo Station, and take either the JR Yamanote or Keihin-Tohoku line to **Akihabara** (¥140/4 mins), the electronics mecca. Browse the electronics shops, pay a visit to **Kanda Myojin shrine**, and visit an anime goods store or two to boggle at the sheer amount and variety of Japanese animation. Stop at

the **Gundam Cafe** for a bite.

If electronics are not your thing, continue your stroll onto **Jimbocho**, the atmospheric used books district, before heading back to your hotel for an early night. If making the tuna auction, arrange a taxi to get to Toyosu Fish Market by 5:15am.

Day Two - Tuesday

Make your way to **Toyosu Fish Market**, to see the tuna auction. You will have a short while before the tuna auction begins, after which you can reward yourself with a sushi breakfast.

Make your way to Tsukiji and explore the site of the old fish market. Explore the **Outer Market**, browse the goods on offer, picking up a snack or two from the outer market, before heading to

nearby **Hamarikyu Gardens** to recharge while taking in some gorgeous scenery.

For lunch, stroll over to **Ginza**. Head to the **Mitsukoshi Department Store**'s restaurant floor, and pick one of the many restaurants (you can't go wrong with a tempura and soba set meal), before browsing the store for the very best that Japan has to offer. Have afternoon-tea

French style at **Ladurée's Salon de Thé**.

Walk to **Kabuki-za**, the kabuki theatre, to catch some traditional Japanese theatre, before finishing your evening at nearby **Yurakucho**.

Wander the alleys, enjoying the ambiance created by the many lanterns of the yakitori bars and the smell of the cooking meat, before making your choice of restaurant.

Day Three - Wednesday

Head over to **Senso-ji** in Asakusa to enjoy this immensely popular temple before the crowds arrive. Explore the shopping street in front of the temple, but steer clear of the overpriced souvenirs.

Confirm travel plans and get

the latest information from nearby **Asakusa Tourist Information Center** before heading to **Sometaro Okonomiyaki** at 12:00 for some of the best *okonomiyaki* in Tokyo.

Take the Tobu Skytree Line (¥150/3 minutes) to Tokyo

Skytree Station. Spend some time in **Solamachi**, visiting the **Sumida Aquarium** and **Moomin Cafe** before heading up—and up and up—to the **Skytree observation deck**.

Linger, watching the afternoon fade into evening,

and Tokyo's lights emerge, before heading to one of the **Skytree's restaurants** for dinner with a view.

Alternatively, if you want a view of the Skytree with your meal, head to **Teppanyaki Akasaka** on the 37th floor of the Ana Intercontinental Hotel about 30 minutes away.

Day Four - Thursday

Visit **Meiji Jingu Shrine**, then either relax in the park, or rent a cycle while you wait for **Harajuku's** shopping district to wake up. Wander along **Takeshita-dori**, making sure to explore the unique fashion in the side-streets, and to sample one of Harajuku's famous crepes.

For lunch, head to **Omotesando**, where you'll find **Maisen Tonkatsu**, some of Tokyo's best *tonkatsu*, in a restaurant that used to be a public bathhouse.

After lunch, stroll down Omotesando, and **Cat Alley** until you reach **Shibuya**. Take in the iconic **pedestrian crossing** from a coffee shop or Shibuya Mark City, before heading on to dinner in one of Shibuya's restaurants.

If you've still got the energy, stay in Shibuya to sample some of Tokyo's best clubs.

Day Five - Friday

Arrive at Hamacho Station to get to **Arashio sumo stable** by 7:00am, and take in the **morning sumo practice**. When it's finished, take a 25-minute walk over to the **Edo-Tokyo Museum** (open from 9:30). Browse the museum before heading into **Ryogoku** for lunch in one of the many *chanko-nabe* restaurants

catering to the wrestlers.

Head to **Odaiba** (¥540/33 minutes). Get off at Odaiba-kaihin Koen and spend the afternoon and evening exploring Odaiba's many attractions.

Don't miss **Teamlab's digital art museums**, and the

Miraikan, **Museum of Innovative Science**, for the robot shows. Once the sun has gone down, take the **waterbus** to Hinode Pier and enjoy the **Rainbow Bridge**.

Once back on dry land, head to **Shibuya Tofuya Utai** for a deluxe *kaiseki* experience - about 15 minutes by train.

Day Six - Saturday

From Sendagaya Station or Shinjuku-gyoenmae Station, head to **Shinjuku Gyoen** for a relaxed start to your day (open from 9:00am). Take this opportunity to try the **tea ceremony** at the park's tea house.

Take the train to Shinanomachi Station. Grab

a *bento* (Japanese boxed lunch) and some snacks from a nearby convenience store, before walking through **Shinanomachi Park** to **Meiji Jingu Baseball Stadium** for a daytime match (starting at 14:00—getting tickets in advance essential).

Head to **Shinjuku** to finish your evening. Explore **Kabuchicho**, dining in one of the area's many *izakaya*, before moving to a bar to finish your night. If the baseball game wasn't entertainment enough, why not try the **Tokyo Robot Restaurant** for an unforgettable experience?

Day Seven - Sunday

Head to **Ueno Park**, visiting Shinobazu Pond and **Bentendo Temple** and **Toshogu Shrine** as well as your pick of Ueno's selection of museums and art galleries.

Grab lunch from a street

stall or one of the many restaurants around the park.

If you've got energy to spare, head to the **Shitamachi Museum** and on to **Yanaka**. Otherwise, stay in Ueno and explore the **Ameyoko Street Market** in

the hopes of finding some last-minute souvenirs.

For dinner, we've saved the best (or at least the most fun) for last: **Ninja Akasaka** which is 20 minutes away by metro.

A Special Thanks

If you have made it this far, thank you very much for reading this guide. We hope this guide will make a big difference to your trip to Tokyo! Remember to take this guide with you while you are visiting this amazing city.

....

If you have any questions or wish to contact us, you can do so at www.independentguidebooks.com. If you have any corrections, feedback about any element of the guide, or a review of an attraction, hotel, area or restaurant – send us a message and we will get back to you.

We also encourage you to leave a review wherever you have purchased this guide from. Your reviews make a huge difference in helping other people find this guide, and we really appreciate your help. You can also leave a little tip to the editor of this guide, buy him a coffee at ko-fi.com/giobooks. Thank you very much!

If you have enjoyed this guide, other travel guides in this series include:

- The Independent Guide to Tokyo Disney Resort
- The Independent Guide to Hong Kong
- The Independent Guide to Dubai
- The Independent Guide to Paris
- The Independent Guide to London
- The Independent Guide to New York City
- The Independent Guide to Walt Disney World
- The Independent Guide to Universal Orlando
- The Independent Guide to Universal Studios Hollywood
- The Independent Guide to Disneyland
- The Independent Guide to Hong Kong Disneyland
- The Independent Guide to Shanghai Disneyland

Have a fantastic time in Tokyo!

Photo Credits:

Photos used under Creative Commons license from flickr: Sengaku-ji - False positives; Narita airport board - nota; Narita Bus - Alession Bragadini; Haneda Airport - Daisuke Tashiro; Airport train and Tokyo Ferry - Hideyuki Kamon; Shinkansen - FuFu Wolf; Bus to Tokyo - tsuda; Tokyo subway train - lucamascaro; Japan Rail - t-mizo; Tokyo subway signs - rich115; Tokyo bus - mdid; Tour bus - OiMax; Tokyo taxi - Mic V.; Driving - Atif Johari; Cycling - Ikusuki; Tokyo Tower - Mustang Joe; Tokyo people with umbrellas at night - Moyan Brenn; Senso-ji - knet2d; Imperial Palace Garden, Kyu Yasuda Teien, Fuji Five Lakes, Nikko Shrine, Oedo Antiques Market, Daiso, Sanja Matsuri and Toshogu Shrine - Guilhem Vellut; Chidorigafuchi - Kanegen; Tokyo Station - kalleboo; Mitsubishi Ichigokan Museum - kubotake; Akihabara - Nakashi; Kanda Myojin - Manish Prabhune; Hie Shrine - kobakou; National Diet Building - Ari Helminen; MOMAT and Tokyo City View Observation Deck - Alexander Svensson; Holy Resurrection Cathedral and Yodobashi Camera Shinjuku - Dick Thomas Johnson; Tsukiji Fish Market - Greg Palmer; Tsukiji Hongan-ji - Manish Prabhune; Hama-rikyu Gardens and Shichi-go-san - KimonBerlin; Kabuki-za - Tom Bennett; Zojoji - Otota Dana; Boat Cruise - wongwt; Odaiba - Antonio Tajuelo; Oedo Onsen Monogatari - Dushan and Miae; Madame Tussauds - Aisyah Hifni; Akasaka Palace - T.Kiya; Baseball Stadium and Shinjuku - Daniel betts; Kabukicho - fletcherjcm; Shibuya Crossing - Candida.Performa; Meiji Jingu - TAKA@P.P.R.S; Omotesando - Andy Smith; Meguro River - Yoppy; Asakusa Culture Tourist Information Center and Ameyayokocho - IQRemix; Ueno Park - Tri Vu Dao; Tokyo National Museum - inu-photo; Shitamachi Museum - Scott Vachalek; Tokyo Skytree - hans-johnson; Ed-Tokyo Museum - Ozgur Cam; Ryogoku Kokugikan (Sumo Stadium) - 'alisdair'; Tokyo Disneyland - 'fortherock'; Studio Ghibli - Travis; Yokohama - 'aotaro' Kamakura - 'Yoshikazu Takada'; Hakone - Paul Robinson; Mt. Fuji - David Hsu; Palette Town - "Richard, enjoy my life!"; Ameyoko - Kim Ahlstrom; Kabukiza - Tom Bennett; Meiji Jingu Stadium (Shinjuku) - Daniel Betts; Ryogoku Kokugikan - François Rejeté; Luxury Dining - Norio Nakayama; Coming of Age Day - Bruce Dailey; Setsubun - DozoDozo; Plum Blossom Festivals - col&tasha; Tokyo Maraton - Naomi Nakashima; Takao-san Fire Walking Festival - 'stan chow'; Asakusa Kannon Kigen-e - J3SSL33; Cherry Blossom Season and Asakusa Samba Carnival Parade - Yoshikazu Takada; Yabusame - Glenn Waters; Kameido Tenjin Shrine Wisteria Festival - Yoshizumi Endo; Kanda Festival, Tokyo Dome, Chrysanthemum Festivals and Omotesando Super Yosakoi - Marufish; Bunkyo Hydrangea Festival - ozma; Tsukiji Shishi Festival - Kent Wang; Sumida River Fireworks Festival - Pietro Zuco; Tokyo Winter Illumination - kouyuzu; Hot pot stew - City Foodsters; Bar High Five - Kent Wang; Night club - dat'; Suntory Hall - Hiroyuki Tsuruno; ACT Theatre - Dick Thomas Johnson